Madness,
Mystery
and the
Survival
of God

Isabel Clarke

First published by O Books, 2008
O Books is an imprint of John Hunt Publishing Ltd., The Bothy, Deershot Lodge, Park Lane, Ropley,
Hants, SO24 0BE, UK
office1@o-books.net
www.o-books.net

Distribution in:

UK and Europe
Orca Book Services
orders@orcabookservices.co.uk
Tel: 01202 665432 Fax: 01202 666219
Int. code (44)

USA and Canada
NBN
custserv@nbnbooks.com
Tel: 1 800 462 6420 Fax: 1 800 338 4550

Australia and New Zealand
Brumby Books
sales@brumbybooks.com.au
Tel: 61 3 9761 5535 Fax: 61 3 9761 7095

Far East (offices in Singapore, Thailand,
Hong Kong, Taiwan)
Pansing Distribution Pte Ltd
kemal@pansing.com
Tel: 65 6319 9939 Fax: 65 6462 5761

South Africa
Alternative Books
altbook@peterhyde.co.za
Tel: 021 555 4027 Fax: 021 447 1430

Text copyright Isabel Clarke 2008

Design: Stuart Davies

ISBN: 978 1 84694 147 4

A CIP catalogue record for this book is available
from the British Library.

Printed by Digital Book Print, www.digitalbookprint.com

Madness, Mystery and the Survival of God

Isabel Clarke

BOOKS

Winchester, UK
Washington, USA

CONTENTS

PREFACE

Experiences, Songs and Poems.

This book is about all the varieties of human experience, not just ideas. So, it was important to illustrate it somehow. As it is about that area of experience that straddles the mystical, the spiritual and the mad, I needed first hand accounts to bring this to life. I approached two people I knew; Annabel I had met at a Scientific and Medical Network meeting, twelve years ago, at the time when I was planning my first book on this subject (Psychosis and Spirituality: exploring the new frontier). Annabel and I are now both part of the development group for the fledgling 'Spiritual Crisis Network' (see list of books and contacts at the end for the web address), and she gives talks about her experiences in order to help others (email contact in references). Starting the Spiritual Crisis Network was an initiative of Catherine's, and she let me use her account of her experience.

I have never met Matthew, but was struck by the account of his much earlier experiences he posted on the Psychosis and Spirituality Yahoo discussion list on the internet. (This list started through conferences that came out of my earlier book – see my web address for more about the list and how to join it, the conferences, and the other things I get up to). I approached him for permission to use it, and as with the other two accounts, am grateful for that permission. I was interested to learn that he since gained his first degree in Anthropology and Management Studies and is currently studying for a BSc degree in 'Psychosocial Interventions for Psychosis'. Presently Matthew is working on an acute psychiatric ward in the NHS, and has continued to develop his spirituality through Buddhist practice. His comment today about these earlier experiences is as follows: 'Although these experiences give an insight which can inform my work, in Zen training such "mystical", "spiritual" or "psychotic" experiences are not the point. In Zen Buddhism the important thing is the activity of zazen (seated meditation)'. Developments in Psychotherapy for psychosis have recently begun to recognise the potential therapeutic value of 'mindfulness' practices (often derived from such Buddhist traditions).

Creativity and humour are vital ingredients of this story. To add these, I turned principally to my two favourite radical songwriters, Robb Johnson and Theo Simon. When the criminal stupidity of the age we live in starts to get to me, the songs produced by these and other relatively unknown 'folk' singers keep me going. The term 'folk' I find misleading. Robb Johnson identifies himself with 'the English Chanson' - but I am not sure that is much better. Theo Simon, with Shannon Smy, leads the collective known as Seize the Day. They are to be found at any climate change demo worth the name, and indeed were present at the notable anti-globalization protest in Seattle. Robb Johnson's radicalism is more in the English socialist (I mean real socialist, forget New Labour....) tradition. They have in common lack of commercial success, despite (because of?) intelligent words, good tunes and an energetic beat. Seize the Day did win overwhelmingly a BBC Radio 3 listeners' vote competition in 2003, but were disqualified because of their opposition to the Iraq war (which the organizers had said influenced the voting!) I give details of Robb Johnson and Seize the Day's CDs and websites in the list of sources and references at the end - do check them out for yourself!

There are a number of other songwriters whose lyrics keep me going, but I was helped to approach these two for permission as I knew they would be able to identify me: Theo Simon because we were both regulars at the protests against the infamous road that demolished Twyford Down (more about that later in the book) – where he would sing his hilarious 'Motorway Song'; Robb Johnson, because I have been a regular fan, turning up at poorly attended gigs, and chatting to him in the interval. I am grateful for their permission, especially as I do not think either of them would be signed up to a straight defence of religion.

The same would go for the other bard represented (apart from a few lines of Rumi at the start of chapter 5), Andrew Jordan. He was another Twyford Down contact, and I can unreservedly recommend his book of poems, 'The Mute Bride', which delicately spins a web of themes around the ancient resonances of that remarkable landscape near Winchester, and its contemporary rape by the road builders.

CHAPTER 1

The Religion versus Science Debate

How do we account for the persistence of religion, the survival of God, in societies shaped and dominated by the triumphs of science? How is it that the thorough understanding of the physical world that modern science affords is not enough for the human imagination? Where does God, and that yearning for the irrational and infinite, fit into the tidy world view of the scientist? The pull of the supernatural and the sacred manifests itself both in the flourishing of religion and through other forms of spirituality, or indeed, superstition. So why have religion, spirituality not conceded defeat in the face of the technological revolution that has transformed our lives and eliminated so much discomfort and uncertainty (at least for those of us in the affluent world)? Why have these reminders of a pre-scientific world view not faded away in the blinding light of scientific logic? After all, science appears to many people to be on the brink of yielding the remaining few answers; the last pieces to slot into the gaps in the jig saw of knowledge.

The rationalist philosophers and writers of the late nineteenth and early twentieth centuries, such as Bertrand Russell and H.G. Wells, along with the ideologues of the communist revolutions of the same era, were convinced that it was just a matter of time before the masses caught up with the scientific vanguard. Their rationalist, materialist successors today, such as Richard Dawkins and Christopher Hitchens, are a little less confident: not in their conviction of the rightness of their position, but in the inevitability of its eventual universal acceptance. They are more irritated than their predecessors of a century ago, and with reason.

With over a century of universal education in the West and even more evidence of the success of science, there has been plenty of time for the masses to fall into line and abandon outmoded superstitions. In defiance of this logic, religion and spirituality are alive and well. They have thrived and multiplied. In some places they might appear to be in decline (for instance, within the sort of liberal Anglicanism tradition that I favour), but overall religions and spiritualities flourish. At the same time, there are suggestions that it is science that could be in retreat. At present (2007) there is a panic in the UK about closures of university science departments and shortages of science teachers in schools; at the same time Creationism is increasingly taught in the English speaking world, in the teeth of scientific opposition. Good cause for irritation and indeed, alarm.

Looking Beyond Debate

This debate has been described in 'science versus religion' terms, because that is how it is often seen and presented. Seen in those terms, one side or the other would have to concede defeat. From my perspective, for either contestant to be eliminated would be a disaster – but, in fact, neither is particularly likely to be obliterated. In what follows, I might sometimes appear to be chipping away at the foundations of science, or undermining religion by association with madness. In fact, I value both as different but essential aspects of the human experience and of human knowing – as I hope to demonstrate.

As a psychologist, I respect and use the scientific approach. I gather evidence and test hypotheses. As a human being, I share the respect for spiritual and religious perspectives that is widespread, even in the scientific community, while recognising that it is not universal. I am not alone in occupying these two positions as a scientist and someone for whom spirituality/religion is important. Eminent commentators in this field have argued from this position that the two realms of discourse should be seen as simply different, as chalk and cheese; and that attempts to reconcile them should be abandoned. The late scholastics of the middle ages opted for this solution. Reconciling Christianity with the embarrassingly sophisticated but resolutely pagan culture of the ancient world, which filtered through to the main centres of Europe in the 12th and 13th centuries CE posed a considerable challenge. The challenge was essentially abandoned when their separate spheres were accepted by the 14th century, after a couple of hundred years of wrestling with the contradictions between theology, the study with the greatest prestige, and Aristotle's obviously sensible logic.

In our own time, the writer on religion and science, John Polkinghorne, for instance, develops this position when writing about physics and religion. Stephen Jay Gould, another commentator in this field, has produced a theory of 'Non-overlapping magisteria' or NOMAs – subject areas that are intrinsically separate and should be considered from within their own frameworks.

This line of argument has certainly not succeeded in squashing the debate. Commentators such as Richard Dawkins and Stephen Hawking who move on from eminence in particular scientific fields to make pronouncements about God are open to the criticism that they have stepped outside their area of competence. Just because they have pushed the boundaries of knowledge with respect to evolution (Dawkins) and cosmology (Hawking) it does not automatically follow that they know everything there is to know about everything. The fact that their pronouncements find a ready audience only supports the contention that I will develop below, that logic and rationality do not in fact reign supreme.

What I wish to argue runs as follows: there are two ways of

talking about the world that are different in character. However, both can be brought into one framework of scientific understanding based on what we know about connections within our cognitive apparatus; the way our thinking is wired up in our brains. My aim is to demonstrate that experimental psychology provides a basis for understanding that sense of connection and relationship with what lies beyond ourselves and beyond what we can precisely know – that is, the whole area of experience we label variously as spiritual, as religious, as supernatural or as sacred. The other side of this argument is more challenging: I will suggest that far from collapsing the spiritual within the confines of the brain, this perspective blows wide open our vision of the human being – wide enough to reach beyond the individual and embrace the infinite. And the key to this perspective is a new way of understanding that other commonplace of human experience, madness and breakdown.

Some Definitions

To start with a some clarification; I am aware that so far I have tended to lump together concepts such as God, spirituality and the sacred in an indiscriminate manner. Set against the sort of anti-religious scientific perspective that labels all these concepts as superstition and would happily consign the lot of them to oblivion, this does not matter. However, each of these terms is contentious in its own right. Without claiming any overall authority for my definitions, I will here attempt to convey what I mean when I use the various terms. This should be taken as a provisional effort. I hope that a richer perspective on these terms will emerge in the course of the book.

I will make some attempt to tackle the thorny subject of God (goddess/gods) in later chapters. Hence, I will skate lightly over this one for the moment, after making two points. Any idea of God or gods/ goddesses etc. involves commitment to the concept of transcendence; that is, the idea that there is something beyond.

It might or might not imply connection or relationship with that beyond. It might or might not have much to say about it. There is a significant divide in this debate between those who adhere to the 'reality' (whatever that means!) of something out there and those who maintain that such a notion is deceptive nonsense. For an entirely un-resolvable argument, this issue generates an awful lot of heat. This is not just an issue that divides the scientific materialist from the spirituality crew. Many people would defend notions of spirituality to the end yet passionately deny any idea of transcendence.

The other point to note here about the god idea is that the major religious traditions, apart from Buddhism, are based on the concept of deity (i.e. God/gods). God goes with organised religion, faith communities and the rest – but as the important exception of Buddhism shows, you cannot even count on that!

Faith traditions, by their very nature, generate teachings, doctrines, beliefs and practices. This body of doctrine and practice will hold the worshipping community together – they provide a framework for communal sharing of the faith. When we turn to the term spirituality, such community practice and doctrine cannot be assumed (but neither can its absence be assumed). Spirituality, I take to be a broader term, referring to a class of experience, and a reaching out in relationship towards the whole. Whether or not 'the whole' implies a 'beyond' is, as I have already indicated, a subject for debate. The term spirituality does not commit itself to specifics about what that relationship is with, but acknowledges the significance of the experience. The term has come into wide usage in recent times because of the very variety of belief, practice and religion found in most societies, at least in the West.

There are a lot of people who have no allegiance to any known faith community, and yet recognize the importance of something that could be labelled spirituality in their lives. This phenomenon provides part of the data that convinces me that this is something worth investigating, and it is very useful to have an umbrella term to refer to. For instance, I work for the UK National Health Service. In the NHS, it is being increasingly recognised that this aspect of people's lives is extremely important, not least when people are facing crises, transitions, ill health and death. However, no universal religious belief or tradition can be assumed; a general term is needed as the first step to sensitive individual enquiry. For instance, the service user driven, 'recovery' approach to mental health, which challenges the expert led, medical model, identifies spirituality as one of the crucial elements that can help someone to get through a mental breakdown and back to good functioning. The recovery approach started in the US and has been adopted by the NHS, and mental health service user movements in the UK. The result has been to put spirituality on the agenda, with conferences, training and questions about it in the standard documentation.

Spirituality, as well as being a very handy, catch-all, term, is also controversial. It has its critics, and those who frankly loath it. The term 'transpersonal' is used in some more specific contexts and finds favour with some who do not like the word spirituality. The specific context that favours the word transpersonal is those schools of psychotherapy that make a feature of the spiritual dimension within their therapy. Unlike spirituality, 'the transpersonal' tends to imply a particular intellectual framework.

What about the term sacred? As I understand it, this term can be approached from two sides. On the one hand, a sacred object, building etc. becomes sacred by association with, or being set aside for religious or other spiritual use. On the other hand it can describe a quality of experience. The emotions associated with such experience are those of wonder, awe and fear. It is an experience of otherness – and this is a subject we will explore at length later in the book.

A Word about Measuring Instruments.

The seductive beauty of the materialistic argument is its simplicity. That which we can see, feel and generally grasp with our senses; what we can measure and manipulate experimentally, is real. The rest is essentially illusory; the product of our imaginations, and though it adds a degree of interest and variety to life, it can be safely sidelined from any serious consideration. This puts consciousness, art, emotion and anything remotely spiritual firmly into its (inferior) place.

The flaw in this argument is its failure to take account of the effect of the instrument of measurement on the conclusion. This is an understandable mistake. When looking forwards it is easy to forget what lies behind us. As we watch the television programme where the famous presenter surveys a desolate desert scene and expands on its emptiness and his vulnerability alone in this wilderness, we are positively meant to forget about the camera crew along with necessary support services. They are safely outside of the picture we see on the screen, but their presence is essential for making that picture happen. In the case of people investigating religion, the camera crew, the instrument of perception and measurement, are ourselves. As a psychologist, this is the bit that interests me.

After all, science inevitably advances along with the development of more sophisticated instruments for exploration and understanding. The invention of the microscope revolutionised biology; new and better telescopes push the boundaries of our conception of the universe. The development of navigational instruments made it possible for people to cross the oceans in sailing ships, discover new continents, and get back to tell the tale. In the same way, the advance of science is held up by the limitations of its instruments. Before the invention of the compass and the sextant ships sensibly hugged the coastline, so the oceans remained unexplored.

There is one instrument that remains the same at the heart of this process - ourselves. It is our minds and our senses that enable us to explore; to reach out to the finest detail of molecular biology and the furthest stars of the galaxy. However, the way in which those minds and senses are themselves constructed shapes the way in which we approach everything we do. This is the part of the great adventure of exploration that it is easy to forget. It is easy to take for granted the instrument that both opens our window on the world, and at the same time imposes a frame that limits it.

I am interested in those limits. I am interested in what the fault lines in the human mind can tell us about the really intriguing questions. About the questions that science, with all its stunning success in subduing nature and creating comfortable lifestyles cannot deliver clear answers on.

Introducing the Construct System

Conventional scientific understanding does recognize an apparatus of theory behind the facts. Theory is introduced by the observer, the camera crew so to speak. The theory is the framework of meaning used to make sense of the facts. A theory is essentially a story – something invented by the human mind. The hard, irreducible facts are important and need to be established, but it is the story we weave around them; the framework of meaning we slot them into and the sense we make of them that is crucial. For instance, many of the facts that supported Charles Darwin's theory of evolution were available before Darwin. His role was to see them in a new light; to tell a new story. Building knowledge is therefore a constant process of gathering data and fitting it into the existing framework, or using it to support a rival theory. Only data that has significance for either supporting or refuting a theory is normally noticed as worthy of collection. This much is well recognized.

There is a psychological theory that neatly explains this rather fundamental aspect of human thought. It was developed by a mathematician who then became a therapist and founder of constructivist psychology in the 1950s, by the name of George Kelly. Kelly was clearly an intellectual with a social conscience, and a real sympathy for his fellow human beings. Though his first line of study had been mathematics and physics, he followed this with psychoanalysis, and found himself working as a community therapist in the 1930s in Kansas – a part of the United States that had been badly hit both by land erosion (the dust bowl phenomenon), and the depression. Theories of Freudian psychoanalysis, the dominant way of doing therapy at the time, seemed and indeed were a world away. He realized that what people in trouble wanted from him was a way of making sense of their situation, and that was what therapists offered.

Kelly generalised this observation into a whole theory of how people make sense of the world, set out in a way that harks back to his earlier training as a mathematician, with postulates and corollaries. The methods he developed for using his theory therapeutically have continued to retain a small but dedicated following. His basic ideas have been enormously influential; for instance, his fundamental approach is clearly visible within Cognitive Behaviour Therapy, probably the dominant therapeutic modality at present, certainly within the UK National Health Service. However, such influences are not necessarily acknowledged or attributed to him.

Kelly saw all people as scientists, doing their best to make sense of their situation by making predictions; forming hypotheses from these predictions and then testing out their hypotheses. These predictions were based on their past experience. Each person develops an individual set of predictions, or constructs, in order to navigate whatever life offers them. The possibilities they have for slotting new experience into the existing framework are constrained by the flexibility or limitations of that framework. The usefulness of the framework for being able to make valid predictions is also affected by how tight or loose it is.

Kelly identified a crucial distinction between rigid, limited, construct systems that might have difficulty in accommodating new information, and very loose construct systems that fail to make valid predictions about anything. My favourite example of a rigid construct system is the response of a young friend of my son's when I offered to make pop corn for the two boys on their return from school together. 'I don't like it. I've never tried it', said the lad with utter conviction – and total ignorance. According to his construct system, the constructs 'new' and 'nasty' overlapped leaving no room for experiment. On the other hand, someone who did not have the 'don't like it' construct at all, could lay themselves open to some very undesirable experiences.

So, our construct systems are built up through past experience, but they also serve to filter and constrain present and future experience. Things that do not fit into the system are filtered out. As well as being individual, construct systems overlap in complex ways; we soak up construct systems around us from our cultural background and the media. Families, social groupings, professions and nationalities hold constructs in common – but can also disagree as individuals.

'Spin' and advertising are about manipulating peoples' construct systems. In this way, things come to appear obvious; it is hard to go against the tide of opinion. The minority view becomes invisible, until effort is put into changing perceptions. I remember a time when refugees were seen as universally deserving of help and sympathy; now the less reputable sections of the media have all but succeeded in painting asylum seekers as scroungers. Once becoming a smoker was almost a right of passage to adulthood. Now it is a pariah habit.

This book will be about laying bare the apparatus of unexamined constructs that support some widely accepted views, and about suggesting new ways of looking at things. I will start by turning the spotlight on a couple of relatively unexamined constructs that make it hard for us to weave a new story. The story I want to weave is the one that can accommodate the scientific along with the sacred, the natural along with the supernatural.

CHAPTER 2

Two Assumptions

As I see it, the way of thinking that regards the spiritual and the supernatural as delusions belonging to a pre-scientific age depends on two normally unexamined constructs. One concerns the relative status of experience and logic as ways of knowing. I will call this the 'rationality' assumption. The other is the assumption that the individual person is complete, self sufficient and shut into their physical being; that we are separate little entities whizzing around and knocking into each other – which I will refer to as the 'billiard ball' model of the person or the 'billiard ball mind'.

The Rationality Assumption.

Let us first examine the assumption that rationality is pre-eminent and more important than experience. This assumption says that where lack of logic and irrationality appear to be in the ascendant, this is simply because of a temporary state of ignorance. Packed within this assumption is the concept of a future golden age of rationality, admittedly not yet attained, but essentially within our grasp. If this is not the direction in which we are heading at the moment, then it jolly well ought to be.

Not everyone is fooled by this construct. The advertising industry certainly isn't. Advertisers rarely set out a couple of pages of closely argued logic in support of their wares. Instead, they appeal to the imagination and the senses. They use association shamelessly, and in other words evoke the rich world of experience to undermine the voice of logic saying; 'Don't waste your money on that rubbish. After all, you don't really need it'.

As a further example, take the mass popularity of 'stars' in our culture. Is the music produced by the latest pop sensation really so sublime as to merit the hysteria and rich rewards surrounding those performances? Or is this yet another example of the irrationality of collective human behaviour. Simple, rational, logic is not in charge here. In fact, in daily life, it is fairly clear which way of knowing; that dominated by rational logic or that governed by the senses and experience, is generally in charge. I am going to argue that both the rational and the sense and experience governed knowing are valid but distinct forms of logic.

Rather than conclude that this more emotional and collective response is somehow inferior because illogical, I will argue that it is governed by that other sort of logic; that other way of knowing that is based on our direct experience. Instead of regarding one as being wrong and the other right, I would suggest that both have their limitations and their strengths. I will base this conclusion on what we know about the limitations and strengths of human information processing through recent advances in psychology. I will further argue, in the next chapter, that this other way of knowing points the way to a different kind of truth, one that has its own validity.

The Billiard Ball Mind Assumption.
The billiard ball mind assumption is the assumption that human beings are self contained within their physical boundaries. In particular, it identifies the mind with the brain and so locates the mind firmly within the skull. Perhaps even more than the rationality assumption, the billiard ball mind falls into the unthinking category of 'the way things are'.

However, there are plenty of everyday examples that violate the assumption. I will be exploring this properly in a later chapter, but for now I will refer to a few instances. The sort of crowd behaviour alluded to above in response to the pop star also holds for football matches, riots etc. The mood, whether of elation and adulation or of menace is catching, and the crowd is 'caught up in it'. Strictly separate, logic governed beings, could not be 'caught up' in this way.

To give another example; in the world of therapy, where I operate, it has been recognised from the time of Freud onwards that whole packages of emotional response 'transfer' from one relationship to another over time; what is known as 'transference'. Formative relations with parents and siblings can shape the way we respond to other people throughout our lives, even if those other people are completely different from our significant, early, figures. In this way the client who is being hostile and defensive with the perfectly reasonable therapist is experiencing their therapist at that moment as if they were a parent or some other important figure. Similarly, while the client recounts horrific events that they have experienced with a deadpan expression, the therapist feels sick, angry and distressed in a way that belongs to the other. For therapy to work, it is important that these phenomena are noted and worked with. In ordinary life it happens all the time with less explicit awareness. How often does the woman say to her partner: 'I am not your mother....'

The Case of Relationship

Relationship is therefore a significant point where the billiard ball mind breaks down. It is also an example of that other type of knowing; knowing that depends on experience rather than objectively verifiable data. Think about the most important relationships in your life. How do you know what they are like? Is your knowledge of the nature of those relationships – whether they are trusting and loving or complex and dissonant, for example, based on observable, physical, objective, data? The stuff of hard science? I suggest that a video camera in your home would be likely to miss the crucial information. That does not mean that your knowledge about your relationships is illusory.

This hard to capture quality of the real nature of relationship, which is after all one of the most important aspects of our lives, goes along with both parties in the relationship being fully specifiable, physical beings. However, not all relationships are with physical beings. Relationship with the football team someone supports does relate to physical beings, but depends on something a bit more than a collection of bodies; the same goes for our relationship with our country. It is just a further step to say that relationship can be experienced in the absence of a physical body. When someone dies, the relationship does not vanish; it remains a part of us. That is what makes the death of someone close so agonizing.

To take this argument a bit further, might not the same go for the experience of relationship with that which is beyond our physical knowledge? An obvious example of such experience is the relationship with God, or another supernatural being. The same could be said of the vaguer sense of the sacred which is a frequently reported experience. Who is to say that this type of experience does not represent *real* relationship? Could it not be argued that the very experience is valid evidence of this truth? The experience of relationship beyond the physical is at the heart of the supernatural.

This argument might appear to require a bit of a leap. I am making a parallel between the ordinary experience of relationship, and purely supernatural relationships. On the one hand, I do recognize that there is a continuum here. A lot of relationships are very ordinary. However, not all – experiences of falling in love, of connection with one's native country, for instance, can attract that magical, mystical quality that is associated with the supernatural. More of this later For now, I want to take the supernatural seriously and unpack this phenomenon in the light of what we know psychologically about relationship and the self.

Taking the supernatural seriously

Where the transferable nature of relationship, and the way in which emotions and mood are 'catching' between people, like infections, is fully grasped, the idea of people as fully self contained modules weakens. The idea of the mind operating beyond the brain, the extendable mind, is not new. Some examples: Rupert Sheldrake argued this position in his book called 'The Extended Mind'; the model of mind behind Group Analysis, with its idea of the 'group mind'; Gregory Bateson, the father of systems theory, 's holistic theory incorporates the idea that mind is distributed throughout the system. On the other hand, this position is not generally scientifically accepted. Without the recognition of such a concept there is a real problem for anyone wishing to take the supernatural seriously, especially where it is being linked to the psychology of the brain.

The idea that connection stops with the skull lies at the heart of objections to allowing any sort of reality to experiences of relationship beyond the human and the fully knowable. This is technically called 'transcendence' in religion-speak. The billiard ball mind assumption dictates that any experience of transcendence or the supernatural is simply manufactured by vagaries of the brain; like crackle on the radio receiver, or fuzzy white lines on the TV set.

It can indeed be shown that there are connections between brain activity or particular areas of the brain and spiritual experience. After all, everything in our perception and thought processes is underpinned by things happening in our nervous system, so that it would be surprising if this area of experience was the exception.

Temporal lobe epilepsy is a case in point. Mystical experiences, that is ecstatic experiences of oneness with the universe, do occur as a result of this condition. This connection caused a bit of a stir in 1997 when researcher Steve Connor claimed that this phenomenon led to the identification of a 'God spot' in the brain. This was followed up by Michael Persinger's special helmet, designed to stimulate this region, which enabled him to induce mystical experiences in some of his subjects. I will return to the debate that followed and subsequent research in a later chapter. For now, I will let the famous 19th century Russian novelist, Dostoievski, who suffered from such epilepsy, illustrate this point from the following example from his famous novel, 'The Idiot'. Dostoievski gives Prince Myshkin, the 'idiot' (or, perhaps, 'innocent') of the title, his own condition, and describes it in the novel as follows:

> He was thinking, incidentally, that there was a moment or two in his epileptic condition almost before the fit itself (if it occurred during his waking hours) when suddenly amid the sadness, spiritual darkness and depression, his brain seemed to catch fire at brief moments, and with an extraordinary momentum. His vital forces were strained to the utmost all at once. His sensation of being alive and his awareness increased tenfold at those moments which flashed by like lightning. His mind and heart were flooded by a dazzling light. All his agitation, all his doubts and worries seemed composed in a twinkling, culminating in a great calm, full of serene and harmonious joy and hope, full of understanding and the knowledge of the final cause. But those moments, those flashes of intuition, were merely the presentiment of the last second (never more than a second) which preceded the actual fit.) This second was, of course, unendurable.
>
> P.258. Dostoievski. 'The Idiot'. Translated by David Magarshack.

I will be linking connections within the brain and this sort of experience in a later chapter. Seen through the lens of the billiard ball mind assumption, discovering these sort of neuro-psychological correspondences with particular experiences reduce all spiritual and transcendent experience to some peculiarity or malfunction of the individual's nervous system. This type of logic argues that because there is an adequate neuro-psychological explanation for an experience, the reality of the perceived connectedness is ruled out.

Both – and logic

I will here introduce an argument that will recur as a theme throughout the book. The way of knowing that is about experience, relationship and connectedness is characterised by a logic of 'both – and'. Ordinary rationality is built on a logic of 'either-or'. Scientific logic tends to assume that if one adequate explanation has been found, all competing explanations are ruled out. Temporal lobe epilepsy can produce mystical experiences, hence mystical experiences are some sort of special case of epilepsy. I hope to show that this is not the only logic to govern human affairs, and that in this subject area, we do well to loosen up enough on our construct systems to allow for this sort of double explanation.

An Example from Psychosis

Another example of how the two logics; that of 'either-or' and that of 'both-and' can deal differently with the same phenomenon can be found in psychotic experience. People who have crossed the boundary into what is popularly known as madness, and which is called psychosis, in a more technical sense, frequently report the experience of being possessed by another person or being. This experience is also associated with certain forms of charismatic religion, and is taken more seriously in some traditional cultures than in our own society.

As a therapist working with people with these sorts of problems, I can often, in collaboration with the individual, forge links between their particular possession experience and difficult experiences, traumatic happenings or abusive relationships in their life story. Such links often suggest to me that the particular experience is the product of unresolved issues within the person's psyche. I will discuss this idea with the individual, and if it makes sense to them, it can often be helpful.

At the same time, I do not rule out the idea of possession, either in the case of this individual, or in general. I think that there is enough evidence that the contents of minds can transfer from one person to another to take the possibility perfectly seriously. Other such evidence is provided by reports of past life regression and the phenomenon of channelling. I have a model of the organisation of thinking, to follow in a later chapter, which allows for this to happen. I also have enough respect for the complexity of this area of experience not to be too certain about anything. This is a case where constructs need to be flexible enough to allow for several possibilities, while tight enough to enable making sense of the experiences, even if this sense-making is provisional.

To conclude, the subject matter of this book is religion, transcendence and the supernatural. I argue that consideration of neuro-psychology, cognitive organisation, and madness are part of a thorough exploration of these subjects. However, I do not bring these different realms of discourse together in order to undermine the ideas of transcendence or the supernatural, but rather to find a new framework that can accommodate all these aspects of human experience.

Recognizing that the either-or logic of rationality, and the billiard ball mind are each one way of construing, and not the only one, opens the way to a wider vista, a broader horizon. From this new vantage point, our minds are no longer just there to steer the individual in his/her separate space. They exist in connectedness and relationship, and this connectedness and relationship is an integral part of what we are. The fact that connection beyond the limits of what is precisely knowable has been a common experience throughout human history, and is an experience that continues to be reported today, suggests that it should not be dismissed lightly. Such reports imply that our capacity to connect and be in relationship operates beyond our connections with our fellow creatures on this earth, human and non human. I will argue that this wider sense of connection is significant for our well-being and for the well-being of the planet.

I will conclude this chapter with the first two verses and the chorus of a song by Theo Simon (see the Preface for information about my choice of songs and poems.). This song light-heartedly illustrates a non billiard ball perspective on the human being, and offers plenty of examples of 'both-and' thinking about our place in the cosmos.

Child of the Universe.
Here's a little history
of a bigger mystery
I have written this story
into my song.
If it
isn't what you're used to
I hope it will amuse you,
and maybe if you choose to
then you'll sing along.
It goes:

I am as old as the universe:
I've been here before
and I'll be here again.
I am a child of the universe:
a part of all women
and a part of all men.

Once upon a sometime
and once upon a somewhere

and once upon a somehow
there was a big bang.
Energy revolving
and energy dissolving
and energy evolving
and that's what I am.

I am as old ...

Theo   Simon.   Seize   the   Day. From   the   CD   'Alive',
www.seizetheday.org

CHAPTER 3

Truth and Myth

The Role of Story.

In chapter one, I introduced the idea of constructs and story. In chapter two, I started to outline a new story about the human being. This is a story that includes all that we can discover from scientific investigation of the brain and our apparatus of thinking. It also takes seriously the information that human beings have collected from experience in important and interesting areas such as relationship, the supernatural, and madness. It is a story that presents us with two very different ways of making sense of the world; that which is governed by 'either-or' logic and that which is governed by 'both-and logic'. It also presents us with two distinct and not entirely compatible models of the person. The self contained individual and the person awash with influences, pulled hither and thither by relationship and emotion. How can I hope to get away with anything so disjointed and untidy?

My answer is to question tidiness. Tidiness that ignores part of the data in order to present a neatly packaged account does not do justice to truth. As I hinted in the earlier chapter, along with recognizing two ways of knowing, I respect more than one way towards grasping truth – or more than one sort of truth. Science necessarily aims at neat and tidy theories, which at least for a time, until they are challenged, make straightforward sense of the facts. Myth and story are earlier ways, relied upon by our pre-scientific ancestors, to make sense of the world and reveal truth. The rationalist tradition of the preceding centuries has downgraded this way of seeking after truth.

Things that do not fit easily into the dominant story are invisible or easily dismissed and the importance of this level of story or meaning-making tends to be glossed over in our culture. When we take into account the power that our construct systems, both individual and collective, hold over our perceptions and conclusions, we can see how story, myth and frameworks of meaning become as important for our sense of what is out there as the verifiable facts.

Despite this, the dominant culture tends to be blind to this role of story. The truth of myth, of story, of poetry and art is accepted, but given an inferior role compared to the truth of science. The dominant, scientific, culture is convinced that while fact-based truth is 'true' in an absolute and objective sense, the other one is true in a relative and subjective manner.

A Framework for Contradiction

My task is to provide a framework to contain untidy and contradictory information about knowledge and about human beings. In other words, we need a new story that does justice to the contradictions and does not try to pretend that they are not there. The part of our minds that wants to be in control is disturbed by contradictions and would like to find a way of reconciling them. A central argument of this book is that these contradictions are written deep into our psyche. By accepting contradictions and holding them in tension, myth and story can manage that sense of mystery that ordinary logic would like to eliminate.

Science is accustomed to ridicule myths as inadequate and bungling attempts at scientific explanation. However, science depends on theories as a framework for gathering and accommodating the data it collects. Theory and story can describe much the same thing – a coherent account that puts things into place. As scientific theories are modified, updated and superseded, science comes to look a little less like a straight description of 'what is' and more like a set of constructs, to refer back to the Kelly's theory of how we think. Newton's world view was updated by Einstein's. Parapsychology data, despite high standards of scientific rigour in its collection, is fiercely resisted, downgraded and denied, because there is no respectable scientific narrative into which it fits.

Similarly, religion ties itself into knots when it tries to claim that its myths are true in a scientific or historical sense. The attempts to fit the very solid data on the age of the earth into the myths of the book of Genesis in the Christian bible are one example of this type of confusion. This is an example of an attempt to resolve the un-resolvable. Like scientific scorn at mythic creation accounts for doing incompetent science, this futile endeavour attempts to gloss over the reality of the two ways of knowing, the two types of truth. This is the area of muddle where myth and story come into their own. In dealing with the un-resolvable, with paradox; with contradiction where neither party will yield, we need myth.

So, in seeking to grasp the significance of the poor fit between these different conceptions of truth and knowledge, myth can be more helpful than science. As mentioned above, these contradictions are written deep into our psyche. They seem to have been introduced along with the deal that saw us evolve from straightforward apes into complex, language producing creatures. That is the scientific story. The myths that follow take us deeper into this truth, in a way that both sharpens its contradictions and refuses to try to resolve them.

Two Myths

It is characteristic of mythology that important themes echo across different myths from different cultures. Such echoes add weight to individual myths and indicate universal themes that are pointers towards another sort of 'truth' about our situation.

Take the myths of Prometheus, from ancient Greece, and

Adam and Eve from the Bible. On the face of it, very different stories! Prometheus is the hero who, with courage and trickery in equal measure steals fire from the Gods for the benefit of humankind. Divine retribution is hideous - an eternity chained to a rock with his liver pecked by birds - but with the benefit of fire, humankind flourishes.

Adam and Eve are in contrast childlike creatures in relation to the creator God who has placed them in their paradise garden. Naughtily yielding to the temptation to eat the expressly forbidden fruit of the tree of the knowledge of good and evil, the children attempt to shift the blame (Adam: 'it's her fault'; Eve: 'the snake told me to'). Stern father God banishes them from the garden to survive in the real world.

Strip away from these the detailed story-lines with their contrasting characters and a common theme emerges. Human beings have attempted to get above themselves, and what is more, they have succeeded. They have stolen or laid claim to some power that the right order says belongs to God(s) rather than people. The result is twofold; they have attained both godlike power and misery. At the start of the stories we humans are living in the same way as our animal bothers and sisters, with little difference between the human animals and the non-human animals. But then the deed is done. The gates of innocent paradise are closed. There is no going back to the unselfconscious life in the present. Culture and technology set us apart from other animals. The non human animals lack language and have not created agriculture and art, built cities and civilisations. Nor are they threatening to wreck the planet on which we all depend with their activities. Nor do they live daily with the knowledge that one day they will be dead.

Betwixt and Between.

So, our myth-making ancestors were saying something real about the human condition, which both Shakespeare and the writers of the Psalms pointed out. As Hamlet puts it, in a particularly world-weary moment:

What a piece of work is a man! How noble in reason! How infinite in faculty! In form, in moving, how express and admirable! In action, how like an angel! In apprehension how like a god! The beauty of the world! The paragon of animals! And yet to me, what is this quintessence of dust? (Hamlet Act 2, Scene 2).

Or as the psalmist puts it:

What is man that thou art mindful of him: and the son of man, that thou visitest him?

Thou madest him lower than the angels: to crown him with glory and worship.

Thou makest him to have dominion of the works of thy hands: and thou has put all things in subjection under his feet; (*Psalm 8. Book of Common Prayer translation*).

In other words, our condition is that of being straddled, often uncomfortably, between a god and creature. Of course, if I put it like this, I am assuming that the term 'god' is meaningful, just as do the myth developers, Shakespeare and the writer of the psalms. Assuming that 'god' means something is hotly contested in our present culture. Yet, these myths strike a chord, even when God is denied. What are the myths saying that does not depend on the acceptance of god language?

These myths point to themes related to what it feels like to be human that will be picked up in this book. One theme is about being in an uncomfortable place, betwixt and between. We have accepted (by and large) the scientific conclusion that we are jumped up apes. We know that we share most of our DNA, along with many other characteristics with our near, and more distant, animal ancestors. A lot of our priorities are the same: material survival and propagation feature high on the list for us, as well as for the other animals. So does our position in the social hierarchy (if you don't believe me, visualise your next board or committee meeting as a collection of primates; which is the aspiring and actual alpha male, for instance?).

And yet we are gifted or burdened with many features unique to our species. We are blessed(?) with self consciousness that gives us a long view of the fate both of ourselves and our species. We have sophisticated language and tool use that takes our control of our environment and scope for communication far beyond the simple family or tribal group. But that is not all. With all our ability to pin things down precisely with science and technology, our self conscious experience somehow teases us with that which is beyond our grasp. We have stolen the fire or eaten of the fruit - but we are not satisfied; we have lost paradise.

So the underlying themes of these great myths seem to be about gaining something - by distinctly dubious means, and simultaneously paying the price for the acquisition. The price is to be stuck in an uncomfortable place, where the responsibility is more than we can manage and where resolution is just out of reach. Modern science appears to promise resolution, as in the 'science will shortly furnish all the answers' argument; it claims to manage the responsibility when it promises that the technology to overcome global warming is just around the corner. But scepticism kicks in as the really important things remain resolutely just out of reach: things like human relationships working; justice prevailing; the poor being fed; the earth's resources being managed sustainably; the end to war.

These are moral arguments, and morality and religion have always gone hand in hand, although humanists and others argue vigorously that this connection is far from inevitable. Morality inevitably involves tension; tension between greed and responsibility; between individual gain and the good of the collective. The deeper truth that these myths reveal tells us something about the inevitability of tension.

In my view, this ties in well with idea of the two ways of knowing that approach the same landscape from radically incompatible points of view. It is within religion itself that this incompatibility and inner tension can perhaps be seen at its sharpest, perhaps because incompatibility and tension are essential ingredients in that sense of mystery; that awareness of truths that cannot be fully grasped. This will be the theme of the next chapter. For now, I will give the last word to the words of a Robb Johnson song which express that naïve, but sacred, plea for right order, in a somewhat unexpected context.

Father Christmas down Hounslow High Street.
'It's brass monkey weather', says Noddy to Big Ears,
You thank god for the gum boots, the red coat and false beard
Mind you, it smells and it gets up your nose and it's
Six solid weeks of Ho bloody Hos
But the pushchairs dance,
With their Harrys, Kathleens and Daljits
To the beat of Camp Pyerats
Down Hounslow High Street.

You get to the grotto, and that wiffs a bit too,
And Noddy and Big Ears nip off for a quick brew,
And here come the kids with their long list of dreams,
The modest, the greedy, the smilers and screamers,
You follow the guidelines:
No hug, and quick out the door
With some crap made in China
No-one ever asks more.

And then there's this kid.
He's just like all the others.

You say: 'What do ye want?'
He says 'A Po[1] for my brother
And Mummy and Gary to get back together'
You say 'Is that all?'
And he says: 'Well, since you're asking
Fix it so nobody goes to bed hungry;
The fighting all stops;
The sick all get better.'
And he looks at you, smiles, with his nose full of snot
You say 'That's a bit difficult'.
He says: 'No, it's not'.

Robb Johnson. From the CD: 21st Century Blues. Irregular Records.
Last verse omitted.)

---

[1] 'A Po' is one of the 'Teletubbies' - a BBC television programme for very young children or babies.

CHAPTER 4

Religion - a Survival Story

Overnight.

They're moving us on, at the mainline stations,
We must be out of their minds, out of their sight,
No final solution, yet, just my imagination maybe,
But nothing happens overnight.

So where do we go now, with the last bus leaving for Heathrow,
The piss on the stairs, the bloody towerblocks of Babylondon,
Saying our prayers in this age of reason,
Nothing happens overnight.

Overnight, overnight, I don't think the sky will fall,
But would you be there if I called you, overnight?

This long journey home is never-ending,
So where do we start putting things right,
When there are so many hearts that need so much mending,
Nothing happens overnight.

I don't know if the angel will pass over us,
All I know is this, it'll be all right
If we love one another enough,
Nothing happens overnight.

Robb Johnson. From the CD 'Overnight'. (Some verses omitted).

Saying our Prayers in this age of Reason.

'Saying our prayers in this age of reason'; 'I don't know if the angel will pass over us.' This song of Robb Johnson's (which contains a tangle of relevant themes) takes us straight into the survival of religion. At times of stress (like being stranded at the airport at the end of a journey) saying prayers is a response that comes even to people with no wider framework to make sense of the impulse. Similarly, 'the angel will pass over us' carries an echo of meaning. Not everyone will know their bible well enough to recognise the story; the reference to the chilling episode in Exodus where the children of Israel are instructed to smear their door lintels with the blood of the lamb slaughtered for their last meal in the land of Egypt, so that the angel of death, passing through the land and striking all first born males, will 'pass over' the Israelite children. Even without this detail, 'angels' and 'pass over' carry a resonance of something beyond the mundane, a striking contrast with the song's bleak theme of being stranded and pleading for a bed for the night.

So, why do we still say our prayers in this age of reason? On a darker note, why is our world riven with conflict in the name of religion? 'Angel' and 'passover' might come with a cosy other-worldly resonance, but when we examine the story it is far from cosy. The houses of the Egyptians were not 'passed over', so that, according to the story, each family awoke to find their first born child dead. Are these dissonant themes connected? Is there, as commentators such as Richard Dawkins in 'The God Delusion' and Christopher Hitchens in 'God is Not Great' would suggest, something malign about the persistence of religious preoccupation and religious practice? How is it that such themes persist and motivate – to both good and evil ends, in this scientific age? Is it the case of an evil virus to be rooted out as Dawkins would have us think or the misunderstood force for good in the world? Or what?

The fact that we are faced here with stark contrast should come as no surprise. The theme of 'both-and' logic has already been introduced. Engaging with paradox lies at the heart of all religious traditions; it comes in the form of the Zen Buddhist master's exhortation to the disciple to meditate on sound of one hand clapping, in order to help the person break free from the shackles of ordinary reality. Christianity offers plenty of examples of paradox where Jesus attempts to explain the counter intuitive logic of 'the kingdom of God' with enigmatic statements such as: ' And behold, some are last who will be first, and some are first who will be last.'(Luke, 13.30), or ' He who finds his life will lose it, and he who loses his life for my sake will find it.' Matthew 10.39. The subject of peace and conflict provides a clear example of paradox within and between religions.

The major religions have a lot to say about peace. The very greetings and blessings that are used habitually demonstrate this. Shalom (Judaism); Salaam (Islam). The sharing of 'the peace' ('Peace be with you') is central to the communion service or Eucharist in Christianity. The paradox is that religion has always attracted controversy and dissension like no other area of human activity. I would venture to guess that generals from opposing armies could find themselves in more harmonious conversation than the representatives of opposing factions within a particular religion. When the Roman Emperor, Constantine decided that it would be politically expedient to adopt Christianity, he initiated the process that would end up with its adoption as the state religion of the Roman Empire under Theodosius. The political authorities of the Empire then found that they had a major task on their hands to knock heads together over the hornet's nest of disagreements over doctrine between the various Christian factions; the result of the official ultimatum that they get their act together and sort it out are the major Christian creeds.

In this chapter, I will argue that this controversy and passionate disagreement, that is to be found within all the major religious traditions, to say nothing of the relations between them, is all part of the fundamental gulfs between types of truth and knowledge explored in the earlier chapters. Far from being a way of escaping from the uncomfortable and the unresolved, religion finds itself at the sharp end of all the rough edges of being human. Religion is in its nature about trying to grasp the intrinsically ungraspable. It is about reaching after mystery. It must, therefore, always reach beyond ordinary logic, but because human beings are logical creatures, they will always seek to bring ordinary, either-or logic to bear on it. Time and again, religion is snagged by 'the rationality assumption' that lurks like a hidden, underwater, obstacle in a shipping lane - that is where the problem lies! On the other hand, this rootedness of the religious and spiritual in the other logic, the other way of knowing, helps to explain its survival in the face of challenge from scientific argument; that persistence illustrated by the phenomenon of 'saying our prayers in this age of reason'.

Getting to grips with God

Efforts to get to grips with the concept of God are particularly prone to snagging by the rationality assumption. Innocent sounding questions such as; 'does God exist?' place the conversation firmly in the realm of factual, logical, knowledge. This is a realm that has very little to say about God – possibly nothing. Ask a different question: 'do human beings report experience of God? Do they reach out to God in relationship, in worship, in supplication?' and the answer has to be that they often do. According to the rationality assumption, in doing so they are deluded. The argument of this book is that our reason does not know everything. Often, the things reason misses are the most important things. Because we can experience more than we can precisely know, it is legitimate to take this phenomenon of reaching out to God, this responding beyond the bounds of rationality, seriously. This is the sphere of 'mystery', and our impatient, rationalist, age can be intolerant of mystery.

People have attempted to 'prove' the existence of God, from St. Anselm and St. Thomas Aquinas in the Middle Ages onwards. Those proofs have only appeared convincing to those who already believe. I hope to show how this is inevitable. Scepticism about God can be accepted as entirely logical. Personally, I have some certainty around what happens to 'me' after death... I am certain that I have absolutely no idea. The concept of 'my' individual survival makes little sense to me personally, but for those who believe otherwise, I can only venture that their guess is as good as mine. The data are simply absent. On the other hand, I would label myself as a 'religious person'. I attend my Anglican church regularly. The services tend to induce in me a constant state of irritation, which I accept and am essentially content with. I accept that connecting with the mystery is an essential for me, but that, because it is mystery, all attempts to spell out the details of it are bound to jar. It is like the episode of the BBC radio comedy 'Radio Active' on 'The Unknown'. The presenters promised to reveal everything that was known about 'the unknown' - namely, absolutely nothing.

We are back to the sense of discomfort and unease introduced by the myths in the previous chapter. Uneasy relationships and religion go hand in hand. At the heart of it lies the tension between precise, verifiable, factual knowledge, and the sense that everything really important in human life, such as relationships and value, somehow slips down the cracks between the logical certainties. In terms of God, there are glaring tensions - between God and precise knowing, and between experience of God, or religious experience, and religion.

Naming God

So, what do I mean by God? That would be telling! My hope is that you will have some sense of the answer to that question if you are drawn to persist with the journey of this book. The trouble is that the question itself hits an immediate paradox.

'God' is obviously a word. The word is used to describe a concept - an idea that is shared by people; an idea on which there is a measure of agreement, and so in need of a word to describe it. However, when it comes to definition, the greatest measure of agreement among authorities is that this is a concept that defies definition.

All the major religions hold to the essential unknowableness of God. In Judaism, the very naming of God is forbidden as blasphemy. 'Yahweh', or 'I am that I am' is surely a refusal to name. What is known as the Apophatic tradition in Christianity 'defines' God by stating what he/she is not. Islam could appear to be the exception here with its ninety-nine names for God. However, these are descriptors or attributes (such as the merciful, the beautiful), not definitions. 'Allah', the real name, makes no comparison, and so says nothing. Behind the many gods of Hinduism is an underlying principle referred to simply as 'that'; in other words, explicitly not named. Buddhism goes furthest in distancing itself from a conceptualised God.

We have hit another paradox. Many words are spun, names are generated and a vast area of study is devoted to a concept which is inherently unknowable. So, where do all the tomes on theology and scripture come from? They come from all the schools and universities throughout the ages studying religion and theology. What about religious practice and religious institu-tions? Societies and cultures throughout history have centred themselves around their religion. They have poured their material resources into it to the extent that any archaeological excavation of an unknown ancient civilisation encountering the remains of a particularly large, magnificent and richly adorned structure will conclude that this is a sacred building. Art, architecture and music have taken much of their inspiration from religion. Surely it cannot all be about nothing?

This paradox points, again, to the central argument of this book, which draws the distinction between two distinct types of knowing - knowing about; logical, scientific knowing; and knowing through experience. These two are often confused. Knowing through experience is frequently not taken seriously because it is not objectively verifiable. This failure to recognise that there are two ways of knowing, and the downgrading of the experiential one, leads to much of the tension between science and religion - and indeed to many of the aberrations of religion itself. In later chapters I will be exploring the way in which these two ways of knowing arise from the very organisation of our brains. For the moment, let us see how these two; the inner and the outer knowing, sit together in the context of religion. The answer can be expressed in one word - uneasily.

Inner and Outer religion: my experience.

To start with my own experience of the distinction between inner and outer knowing in the context of religion: anyone reading the first bit of this chapter could be forgiven for wondering why on earth I bother to go to church, given that I am indifferent to or sceptical about an afterlife, and frequently feel at odds with what actually goes on during the services. The answer is that it feels important for me to connect with that side of my experience. I am a religious person. Is that because of my upbringing? Not really. My father (the parent I identified most closely with) was a scientist and a lifelong atheist. My mother, who came to England from Vienna as an adult, and who was also brought up by an atheist mother, started to go to church when my (elder) brother was confirmed in the context of school.

As the youngest member of this small family by seven years, I was the most serious about religion. The spiritual side of life just 'felt' important, and attending church was a way in which I could honour that, along with contemplating with awe the Austrian mountains where we spent our holidays, or the shapes made by the clouds above our Surrey garden. At the same time, scientific influences in that family were strong. They were represented by my father and my idolized elder brother. The desire to get to grips with this mismatch between the scientific and the religious has been with me for most of my life.

So, from an unrepresentative sample of one (me) I conclude that the spiritual sense that people experience is one strand in the persistence and flourishing of religious observance. This felt sense varies from my own, rather vague, receptivity to 'the spiritual', to the sort of profound and unsettling experiences of opening to another 'dimension' that I will return to in the next chapters. However, in making sense of the success of faith communities I am aware that cultural, tribal and political factors also play their part. The personal, felt experience strand, does not necessarily sit easily with the religious institutions that faith communities develop. Inner and outer religion/spiritualities are the sort of partners that cannot do without each other, but cannot live in harmony either. They vie for dominance. Sometimes one appears on top, sometimes another. They appear to divorce at times, but always get back together in a different form. This is another of those cracks; those uneasy, disjointed places in the human condition, where, try as we may, things don't add up.

The tension starts with the origins of the major religions that dominate the present spiritual landscape. These faiths were founded by individuals with profound personal experience of an ultimate reality, beyond the ordinary, which might or might not be made sense of in personal terms and labelled as God. Moses met God on the mountain, and his face shone as a result of the encounter. Buddha experienced enlightenment. Jesus received his calling through the experience at his baptism. Mohammed took dictation from God. In contrast to the many other people who feel themselves to be divine, or uniquely commissioned from God, these claims were accepted by close followers and then mass movements. In this way, religions are founded.

It would be tidy if these recognized religious leaders were the only people to have this sort of experience. The rest of us would then constitute 'the flock' to use the Christian term. Like sheep, we would obediently follow the divine or divinely inspired teacher. I suspect that religion would not have survived for very long if that were the whole story. In reality, many people experience, in the course of their life's journey, encounters with what appears to be a reality beyond, encounters with the divine. Many experience this as a commission from God - or, more subversively still, a message that they are God or the equivalent.

These encounters can be ecstatic. They can be disturbing and destabilizing. Like the experiences of the prophets in the Jewish scriptures (the 'Old Testament' of the Christian Bible), they are frequently both. These types of encounters will be treated in depth in later chapters, but for now, the point is that such direct experience of the divine is not always comfortable for established faith communities. In Christianity, the line between saints and heretics has often been a fine one. Prominent Christian mystics such as Meister Eckhardt and Jacob Boehme came into conflict with the church authorities, concerned to preserve the purity of doctrine. Some members of the mystical branch of Islam, the Sufis, wear their distinguishing badges hidden, for fear of their fellow religionists.

Morality and values

The inner and outer experience of religion can also lead to unease in the context of morality and values - that other essential ingredient for any authentic religion or spirituality. The 'natural' order of the primate (in the sense of ape) hierarchy works on the principle of 'might is right'; the strongest prevails over the weaker. Religious order turns that on its head. For most branches of the major faiths, the ideal set before people of faith for them to follow is one of justice and compassion for the weak. There is a sacred duty towards the poor, the needy and those outside the protection of the settled society, (the orphans and widows, the stranger and the alien), and even outcasts such as prisoners.

In Christianity, the marginalised have a particular role in leading the way for the privileged, along with themselves, towards the kingdom; the kingdom is the ideal state of being towards which the leader of the faith is drawing his followers. This highly social morality of the Abrahamic religions is not always convenient for the elite within religious structures, and they respond with a drive to frame morality in terms of individual 'purity' - producing another area of tension, this time between ritual purity and the justice tradition. Religions, and sects within religions constantly balance and rebalance themselves between these poles. In my own journey of faith, the Creation Spirituality prophet, Matthew Fox, was important in showing me how the justice tradition applied to the plight of the earth, as well as emphasising that role of the marginalised in the Christian tradition. The movement that was inspired by his talks and writings (for instance, the book 'Original Blessing') is now called GreenSpirit, and is the important other strand in my spiritual life.

In learning about Jesus from reading the first three gospels of the New Testament of the Bible, I am continually struck by the way Jesus champions the uncomfortable and uncompromising social morality. He makes no bones about accusing the religious institutions of his day, which were in the grip of the power elite, of undermining this morality. His verbal battering of the representatives of those institutions was virulent ('you poisonous snakes: you tombs, whitewashed on the outside but full of decay inside') and spilled over into direct action when he laid into the display stands of the money changers in the temple... These are the words and deeds of the founder of a religion who, by implication, constantly challenges those who hold positions of comfortable superiority in the church founded to perpetuate his message. Here is a tension that goes to the heart of the institution of the church. My grumbles at the sermon and the words of the liturgy pale by comparison.

This example comes from Christianity as that is the faith I am

most familiar with, but similar tensions abound in other traditions. Also, there is something about the centralized way that
Christianity tends to be organized that invites conflict between
individual vision and the party line. However, other faiths also
have their difficulties with the unorthodox vision of the mystic.
The uneasy relationship between Sufism, its mystical branch, and
the rest of Islam has already been alluded to.

So, religions are founded by visionaries who have journeyed
further than most into the unknown and unknowable territory of
mystery, and have returned with teaching about this mystery,
about value and about morality, teaching which has been
received and propagated, and has then become institutionalized.
This process is riven with paradox and tension. Later chapters
will establish ways of talking about the visionary state that lies
behind the religious impulse in general, and behind the extreme
experiences of the prophets and founders of the religions. Once
we have a clearer grasp of this elusive area of experience and
ways of talking about it, the next stage of the journey will be to
follow visionaries from our own day, people who have
penetrated further into this strange territory than most. We will
follow them to extreme experience; experience that was ecstatic
and hopeful for humankind. We will also follow them through
experience that was terrifying and incomprehensible. We will
follow them to madness and the asylum.

CHAPTER 5

'The doorsill where the two worlds meet'

The breeze at dawn has secrets to tell you.
Don't go back to sleep.
You must ask for what you really want.
Don't go back to sleep.
People are going back and forth across the doorsill
Where the two worlds touch.
The door is round and open.
Don't go back to sleep.

Rumi, translated by John Moyne & Coleman Barks in 'Open Secret'
(Threshold books).

A New Word for an elusive idea.

It is time to explore more deeply that non rational, visionary quality of experience. The hold that religion, spirituality and the supernatural has on the human mind is bound up with this type of experience. It is that hold on the human mind that this book seeks to explore.

As we have seen in the previous chapter, encounters of this type are the stuff of the origins of religious and spiritual movements. I will further argue that they are equally the stuff of madness. In this chapter I want to establish a firmer picture of what can be a rather diffuse and woolly concept. This imprecision is partly to do with the hard to grasp nature of the subject. However, the inadequacy of the language that we have for talking about it bears its share of responsibility. In order to do justice to this important subject, I propose to introduce an unfamiliar term to describe it.

Introducing a new word is not something I do lightly. There are quite enough words around already. On the other hand, there is a problem with words. Granted, they are very useful and convey the sense you want to get across if chosen aright. But at the same time, they slip in several other meanings that you had not necessarily even thought of.

Words do two things: they distinguish things cleanly, which is the foundation of our success in science and technology. But, equally importantly, they make associations, and so muddle things up - and the result is richer but less precise. Poetic language depends entirely on this association facility. (The two functions of words depend on a fundamental split in the processing pathways in our brain that I will be explored thoroughly in later chapters). The only ways to minimise this effect are to use precisely defined, technical language, or very careful definition or choice of terms. I consider that much of the confusion around the subject area covered in this book has been slipped in along with the terms used. I propose to do a little unscrambling.

It is not as if no-one has talked about this sort of thing before. They have, and to do so they have used words - different and often contradictory words. For instance, the terms that the psychoanalysts and psychodynamic theorists would use in this discussion are: 'subconscious' or 'unconscious'.

So, what is wrong with the word 'unconscious', a word particularly associated with the early psychoanalyst most interested in the religious and spiritual dimension, Carl Gustav Jung? I like the term 'unconscious'. I like Jung's work - it has been an enormously helpful influence on my thinking. I particularly like the idea of the collective unconscious, and will return to that later. But...it is those associations - ideas the word lets in, and other ideas that it excludes. 'Unconscious', for me (and the realm of associations is necessarily personal and imprecise) conjures up waking out of sleep; moving forwards from a regressed place into a more realised and awake one.

This is because this term does have a rather specific technical source in the practice of psychoanalysis which restricts the range of experiences associated with it. 'The unconscious' brings to mind remembered dreams, free association, and revelation of the subterranean workings of the mind through the interpretation of the analyst. The problem is that this does seem to relegate the experiences of the great mystics to the status of dreaming. Worse, it is much too close to Freud's version of the concept, the 'subconscious'. 'Sub' takes us down into subways, the underground and inferior. That is simply unacceptable. So I want something a little more elevated. And besides, strictly speaking, by definition, if something is unconscious, we should know nothing about it - so be unable to say anything about it.....

What else has the dictionary to offer? What about 'transcendent'? I am afraid I am going to turn my nose up at that too. True, it is perfect for mystical experience, but, despite the fact that 'trans' means across, it has acquired an elevated, 'ascending' feel, so just does not feel right for psychosis.

I don't want to go up or down, with all the values associated with those directions. I want to go somewhere else; into another dimension; at the same time, I want to stay right here. So I am going to use 'transliminal' which means 'across the threshold' or 'through the doorway'. It was first used by Michael Thalbourne, and taken up by Gordon Claridge, whose work I talk about later. To my mind it is perfect, and being unfamiliar, it has not had time to acquire any baggage. That won't last, of course.

Of course, the doorsill or threshold is another concrete image - you can see it; it might be the boundary between your house and the outside world at the front door, or simply the line between two rooms within a building with a door between them. This image has both its usefulness and its limitations. A major plus from my point of view is that it corresponds reasonably closely to what I think happens in information processing terms in the brain.

Getting a picture of the transliminal

I will cover this information processing aspect in detail in a later chapter but will explain what I mean for the moment: the two ways of knowing are based on a constant switching between two information processing modes in the brain, where one or the other can be temporarily in charge. Technically, this is called buffering. Which of the two is currently buffered will determine which side of the threshold we are operating from. The fact that we normally switch constantly means that we do not usually move very far from the door, and get to explore the room, so to speak. That only happens in the more extreme states.

However, the two rooms do have a rather different character. To play with this metaphor, let us imagine the room on this side of the threshold, the rational room, first. I see it with a desk and a computer; probably strip lighting and functional blinds at the window. The shelves are lined with useful reference books, and there is a sensible chair of the sort that does not wreck the back with long sitting. I can take in all the walls and the window at a glance.

The other room is altogether less clear. It seems to go on for ever, but the lighting, which is filtered to create fascinating textures and a muted range of delightful colours, fails to reveal much about the actual contours of the room or its extent. It does not help that these contours keep changing; what is that glimpse of a vista of endless landscape to that side? Turn the head for a moment and the whole appears quite gloomy and confined. What is that sinister shape lurking in the darkest corner? The furniture is similarly non-functional and unstable of state.....

As with all images, this little fantasy of interior design has its usefulness and its limitations. As a picture of the human condition, it is important to remember that we spend our time flitting back and forth between the two rooms, and normally, we never get to settle down in either of them. This does not sound very restful. Recall at this point the distinctly uncomfortable picture of the situation of humanity given in the two myths quoted in Chapter 3; banished from paradise or eternally chained to a rock. Dodging from room to room is not quite as bad as that, but this does appear to be a further example of the discomfort and unease theme.

What is useful to remember from this image is that the mysterious room is always around; we keep nipping into it; its influence seeps into the other one – perhaps some suspect books creep onto those tidy shelves? The odd richly decorated cushion might find its way onto that functional chair?

These two aspects of human experience correspond to the two ways of knowing introduced in the earlier chapters. The functional office represents the rational, either-or logic, way of knowing. The mysterious room with no clear limits corresponds to the relational and emotional, way of knowing that is based on experience. From now on I will refer to this aspect of experience as the transliminal, and the other as the everyday.

Tracking the influence of the transliminal

In diluted and manageable form, the transliminal is very much part of the stuff of everyday life. It is present in those things that appeal to our imagination and emotions – as the advertising industry has noted and cashed in on. It is there in the sense of wonder and mystery which accompanies important encounters; encounters with nature or with art. Or it could be the sense of grasping a fuller version of 'the story' whether through a more convincing scientific theory or a revealing myth for our time. As such, it is present at all those 'magic' moments – the times that make life worth living and give it colour and joy.

However, all is not sweetness and light with the transliminal.

It is a place of extremes. The manner in which the transliminal-dominated way of knowing works by association can have powerful but poorly recognised effects. I will illustrate this with another advertising example. In 'No Logo', her devastating exposure of the process of globalisation over the previous decades, Naomi Klein tracks the way in which brands were divorced from their roots in local manufacturing, using this very power of association.

A brand such as Nike was constructed to draw its attractiveness from the human hunger for status and peer acceptance. By associating it with sporting prowess and 'cool' it would be accepted as a passport to those desirable attributes. Obviously this association works in flat defiance of any ordinary logic. The brand was designed deliberately to exude the sort of magic that would transform an insecure teenager into a confident star. This dazzling image, wrapped into the logo, served to conceal and cast into the shade the dark side of the operation. That dark side was the closing down of manufacturing in the developed world and its transfer to places where exploitation of labour and pollution could occur unchecked. As the newly glamorized products could command inflated prices that bore no relation to the depressed cost of manufacture, profits could go through the roof.

So, the transliminal works its influence upon us all the time, sometimes painting otherwise ordinary life in more vivid colours; sometimes laying us open to manipulation. We cannot get away from it. It is part of the fabric of our being, and it tends to beckon us, to invite us further into that infinite and mysterious room. How much of normal activity is governed by that attraction? Losing oneself in a good book, the alternate reality of a film or a soap opera is one common example. Switching off that relentlessly sensible, rational way of knowing with a glass or two of alcohol is another. And there are substances that can take people further into that other room...

The transliminal and mystical experience

Clearly, these rather banal examples are different in kind from the extreme forms of the transliminal as it is encountered in the mystical and prophetic experiences that lie at the root of the religious traditions. Such experiences can occur spontaneously. I have cited an example of such an experience as recounted in a novel by Dostoievski, whose epilepsy opened him to such encounters. However, all religious traditions have mystical, esoteric or contemplative branches that study this aspect of experience. There are centuries of accumulated wisdom in these traditions that teach how to access the transliminal safely, and how to use its gifts in a positive and balanced manner. The dangers lurking in this sort of exploration are well recognised in these communities of meditation and prayer. The technology has been developed for managing the dark side of the transliminal: uncontrollable, terrifying states in which the individual can become lost in madness. Nevertheless, there are no absolute guarantees.

There are differences in emphasis within these various traditions. Some value the actual experience more highly than others, though most see it as a means to an end; not something to be sought or lingered in for its own sake. Others devote their lives essentially to this other way of experiencing; to relationship with God, or however they conceptualise the ultimate within their tradition. We shall visit some of these in the next chapter.

CHAPTER 6

A Scattering of Saints and Visionaries

Most religions have devotees who withdraw from the world and dedicate their lives to their faith or tradition. This leads to rich literature about the transliminal journey. Buddhism is particularly strong on the practical side of how to enter and manage transliminal states. However, I will turn to the Christian Contemplative tradition to illustrate what I am talking about, as that is the one I am most familiar with.

In the early days, Christians in the Roman Empire (and for practical purposes that meant everywhere) suffered persecution, necessitating a hole in the corner existence or a nasty death (or glorious martyrdom according to how you viewed it). Once this threat was lifted, serious devotees had to face the challenge of how to practice their faith in the midst of ordinary life. It became the fashion to follow the example of Christ and withdraw from the complexities of city life to the simplicity and austerity of the desert. In this harsh environment, serious Christians could better devote their lives to God, and the local population appears to have appreciated this dedication sufficiently to provide them with their modest material needs. Such a life of sensory deprivation and prayer lent itself to visionary experience, both ecstatic and demonic, and the literature of the church fathers (and mothers) bears witness to these experiences. Their success led to followers. Solitary 'monks' (the word means 'alone') soon found themselves anything but alone, and so founded 'monasteries'; a whole tradition of prayerful life, self sufficient and withdrawn

from the world, but appreciated and supported by the wider
society for somehow holding the spiritual line. Austerity, prayer
and rhythmic chanting all encouraged the crossing of the
threshold into the transliminal state. In this way a rich tradition
was born and flourished, both in the Eastern, Byzantium based
church, and in the West. The writings of these mystics have come
down to us, and I draw a smattering of examples from this literature in what follows.

14th Century English Mystics

Over the many centuries and rich history of monasticism, there
were particular flowerings of interest in mystical or transliminal
states. 14th Century England produced one such culture, and
writings produced by the mystics themselves, as well as spiritual
guidebooks for those pursuing this path have come down to us.
The particular flavour of this literature is a strong emphasis on
direct experience of the overwhelming love of God for his
creation, in the context of pain and suffering – both that of Christ,
and of the seeker. They are a lively group of characters, these early
English mystics and mystical writers. There is the eccentric
Yorkshireman, Richard Rolle; the somewhat unhinged Margery
Kemp; the systematizing guidebook writer, Walter Hilton who
produced 'The Ladder of Perfection', and my favourites whom I
will quote, Julian of Norwich and the anonymous author of 'The
Cloud of Unknowing'.

   'The Cloud of Unknowing' was composed as a guide to other
seekers, but strongly founded on personal experience. Unlike
Hilton, and many other commentators in this area, it does not
attempt to map the transliminal territory, but rather stresses its
un-mapability. The writer explains as follows:

   'For of all other creatures and their works, yea and of the
   works of God's self, may a man through grace have fullhead of
   knowing , and well he can think of them: but of God Himself

can no man think.'

He advises the seeker to choose a short word, such as God or Love for his prayer, and then to

> 'fasten this word to thine heart, so that it never go thence for thing that befalleth. This word shall be thy shield and thy spear....With this word, thou shalt beat on this cloud and this darkness above thee. With this word thou shalt smite down all manner of thought under the cloud of forgetting.
>
> ...then, 'If thou wilt stand and not fall, cease never in thine intent: but beat evermore on this cloud of unknowing that is betwixt thee and thy God with a sharp dart of longing love, and loathe for to think on aught under God, and go not thence for anything that befalleth.'

He advises a bare, sparse discipline, and warns against the temptation of sense manifestations:

> ' Ofttimes the devil feigneth quaint sounds in their ears, quaint lights and shining in their eyes, and wonderful smells in their noses: and all is but falsehood.

Julian of Norwich is a particularly attractive figure, both because of the vividness of her writings, and because she gives us a bit more about the context for her visions. She recorded having asked God for a closer experience of Christ's passion, for physical illness and for three 'wounds': of contrition, of compassion and of earnest longing for God. All were granted in spectacular fashion. Seriously ill and expected to die at the age of 30, she experienced 16 revelations or 'showings'. These came to her between the hours of 4.00a.m and 9.00a.m. on 8th May, 1373, with one following the next evening.

The passion of Christ was the focus of most of the 16 revelations, doubtless prepared for by Julian having long meditated on this theme. Despite this necessarily gruesome subject matter, the most striking quality of her testimony is of ecstasy and affirmation. This is illustrated by Julian's most famous saying taken from 'Revelations of Divine Love': 'All will be well, and all will be well and all manner of things will be well.' She reports that Jesus says this to her in answer to her puzzlement about the existence of sin. Where can she fit sin into her experience of the endless goodness of God?

She expresses this experience of God's goodness thus: 'After this God revealed to my soul a superlative spiritual joy. I was filled with the awareness of eternal security, and God powerfully sustained this feeling in me, without any painful fear'. As a medieval Christian, Julian identifies her experiences as a foretaste of heaven, and the 'after this' is worth noting. Her visions of the triumph of love and goodness come in the context of empathically re-experiencing Christ's passion; a giving of herself to a total vulnerability to suffering. She is rewarded with a powerful sense of the underlying goodness of the world.

That fundamental sense of God's love and the paradoxical side of the transliminal is illustrated by another famous vision of Julian's:

> (God) showed me a tiny thing, no bigger than a hazelnut, lying in the palm of the hand, and as round as a ball. I looked at it, puzzled, and thought, 'What is it?'
>
> The answer came: 'It is everything that is made.'
>
> I wondered how it could survive. It was so small that I expected it to shrivel up and disappear.
>
> Then I was answered, 'It exists now and always because God loves it.' Thus I understood that everything exists through the love of God.

St. Teresa of Avila and St. John of the Cross

This theme of ecstatic experience of God's love in the midst of suffering or darkness is understandable in the context of 14th Century England, in the aftermath of the devastating death toll from the recent plague known as the Black Death. Conditions in 16th Century Spain, where my next two mystics, St. Teresa of Avila, and St. John of the Cross, came from were strikingly different. The country was riding on a tide of optimism. Spain had been united under Christian rulers with the defeat of the Moors of Granada, and Spanish fighters had turned their energies from internal conquest to the New World. However, the Catholic church of Spain felt threatened by the Reformation sweeping Northern Europe, so that the monastic context in which our two saints operated was decidedly nervous.

The fact that St. Teresa and St. John were both noted monastic reformers as well as prominent mystical writers is significant. They were operating effectively in the world, and in such politically turbulent times that St. John was imprisoned for nine months, and only gained his freedom by escaping! The way in which a valued role in the world sat well with mystical distinction in those times is also illustrated by Julian's later history. Despite withdrawing to the reclusive life of an anchoress, she was sought out for her wisdom and spiritual direction. This role of hers is illustrated in the account given by Margery Kemp, a fellow visionary, but one who trod that fine line between the mystical vocation and madness. Margery was by her own account an unstable character, given to passionate outpourings and bizarre behaviour. Julian advised her with compassion, and affirmed the spiritual validity of her gift of tears.

Because the pure mystical experience is beyond words and reference points in the world as we know it, the variety of images and metaphors used by the different traditions is interesting. Where I introduced the picture of the two rooms as my way of visualising the transliminal, the more usual image employed in the mystical tradition is of search, journey or pilgrimage.

St. Teresa described her spiritual search as the exploration of an interior castle with its inner sanctuary where God is located. St. John of the Cross used the image of climbing up a mountain – the ascent of Mount Carmel. At the apex of both these journeys is the sense of merging with God; 'the unitive' experience, the highest goal of the mystic. The journey passes from the physical, through the imaginal realm of sights and sounds, to the goal which is pure love. There are parallels here with the Buddhist path towards the non dual, 'One Taste,' experience. Both Teresa and John's images offer promise of this ultimate experience of the divine presence, but with many dangers and difficulties along the way.

St. John describes the encounter with the divine as follows: 'These (divine) touches engender such sweetness and intimate delight in the soul that one of them would more than compensate for all the trials suffered in life.' He is best known for his powerful concept, 'the dark night of the soul', which he explains as follows: 'This dark night is an inflow of God into the soul that purges it of its habitual ignorance and imperfections.....God teaches the soul secretly and instructs it in the perfection of love'. The experience of divine love is so overwhelming that the contrast with human imperfection is almost unbearably painful'.

I would also add that both the dark night of the soul and the cloud of unknowing could be attempts to describe the powerful unease accompanying the move beyond the construct system, to use Kelly's term. The mystics quoted here all pursued a dedicated and disciplined life of prayer in preparation for their journey away from the confining safety of constructed reality. Julian clearly spent years contemplating the passion of Christ before her visions broke upon her. Teresa, John and the author of 'The Cloud' operated within monastic traditions that afforded time and place to prayer, study and liturgy. They were therefore ready to open themselves to this new dimension of experience, and embarked on this exploration with courage. As Julian had prayed for 'wounds', they deliberately and unreservedly made themselves open to experience, whether of love or of pain. Yet, there is a sense in their writings that nothing could have prepared them for the force of the experience; the force of conviction of the love of God that they all took from it, along with the powerful pain of separation or distance, severally described as the dark night or the cloud.

Taking experience seriously

In giving these examples, I am returning to an earlier phase of my own life, when I studied medieval history, and developed a particular interest in the spirituality and spiritual life of that period. Looking back, I recognise that I was attracted to that study just because the Middle Ages were a time when spirituality (and community) were taken seriously. This was in contrast to the intellectual climate of the time, (the 1950s and '60s). As I advanced in age and self confidence, and felt able to tackle real live people, as opposed to the safely dead people of distant history, I studied psychology. I could then embark on the slow process of turning myself into a clinical psychologist.

In my first job after qualification, with a psychiatric rehabilitation department, I was able to offer people who had received, many years previously, diagnoses such as schizophrenia, an opportunity to reflect on their life and experiences. This belonged to the therapist part of my job. What I learnt from some of these encounters started me on the path of exploring, writing and teaching about the transliminal.

I was struck by the accounts that several of those clients gave me of their early breakdown experiences. These had occurred many years previously, but were still vivid in their minds and important for them in how they made sense of their lives. Since that time, everything had gone wrong for them. They had felt themselves to be persecuted; they had been out of control in their behaviour; they had been involuntarily hospitalized; severely medicated for years; and the dreams and promise of their youth had turned to dust.

However, the experiences that some of these clients described at the start of this process matched in every respect the sort of unitive mystical experiences that I was familiar with from my acquaintance with the spiritual literature. I was able to discuss this with them, and was probably the first person to validate these experiences, which had always been dismissed as the first phase of their 'illness'. This in no way led me to romanticise what followed, and the history of personal disaster that had led each of these individuals to be now locked into the mental health system, living in sheltered housing, and without prospect of employment. (This is, of course, far from the inevitable outcome of a mental health breakdown. Such experiences can often be quite short lived, and never repeated, or well managed in the context of a productive life. Because I was employed by a service designed for people with chronic and enduring problems, it was people with chronic and enduring problems that I met.)

I was left with a sense of two irreconcilables; the wonder of the original experience, and the devastation of what happened next. It seemed important to take this sort of experience seriously, whatever its later outcome. While I was pondering these issues, I came across a book that I found enormously exciting and encouraging. This was 'Borderline' by Peter Chadwick. Peter Chadwick, conveniently, had done a doctorate in psychology before having his own massive breakdown experience, which he describes in his various writings with disarming humour and candour. This account excited me because Chadwick's excursion into the other way of experiencing started with an exhilarating sense of overwhelming connectedness and meaning. However, after a few weeks on this high, terrifying paranoia and an uncontrollable drive towards self destruction took over, ending with commitment to psychiatric hospital. It is Chadwick's genius that he was then able to reflect on these experiences and research the area for the benefit of others following the same route. I can thoroughly recommend his more recent account of his experiences in 'Schizophrenia: a positive perspective'.

Finding this account gave me the courage to recognise that what I had noted in my therapy clients pointed to a universal process. It suggested that mysticism and madness could not be kept in separate compartments. They might not always go together, but somehow there was a real connection between them. It seemed that the euphoria of the state of unity with everything, and everything being suffused with meaning, that was first encountered, was somehow linked to the crash that followed. The puzzling and irrational phenomenon of spiritual experiences was therefore connected to the equally poorly understood (to my mind) area of madness. This conviction launched me on the path of seeking to unscramble these connections. In this search I uncovered exciting research findings in the area of overlap between spirituality and psychosis that will be covered in a later chapter. I had the sense that this phenomenon could be the key to unlocking a new understanding of both spiritual experience and madness, if only the phenomena could be anchored in the empirical ground of psychological knowledge.

This conviction was firmly based on the data of the accounts I had heard from the people I encountered as a therapist, together with the data of the (predominantly Christian) spiritual literature I was familiar with, backed up by the emerging body of wider research. Since publishing and running conferences in the area of psychosis and spirituality, I have made contact with a wealth of other people who had stories to tell that paralleled those of my clients and Peter Chadwick, but usually with more benign outcome. If you are to follow me on this journey, it will be necessary for me to present some of this experience data.

Letting experience speak for itself.
So I next propose to hand over to those who have travelled there

in our time, and let some powerful experiences speak for themselves. I hope that these examples will highlight another common assumption to be challenged. This is the assumption that it is possible to distinguish neatly between a nice spiritual experience and a nasty episode of madness. I also hope that they will bring to life what happens when a person enters fully into the transliminal, along with some hints at what that process looks like to the bystanders on the outside.

In deciding how to illustrate this part of my argument with accounts of experience, I had a lot of possibilities to choose between. The spiritual literature of the various faiths are a rich source of accounts from throughout the ages. In England, in our own day, the Alister Hardy Society is dedicated to the collection of just such accounts. A large archive has been accumulated since the 1970s, specifically as a resource for researchers into this area of human experiencing. This archive has a particular emphasis on positive and uplifting experiences, though it does, in fact, represent the whole spectrum, including darker and more ambiguous accounts.

If I had wanted more emphasis on that darker side, I could have requested the co-operation of the people I work with in my daily job in the hospital, as I have for other publications. I chose instead to approach three people who are all, like me, interested in promoting understanding of these matters, and in supporting those who are struggling – that is, struggling both with their own transliminal experiences and also with the stigmatising of that experience by society and the mental health services. Two of these 'experiencers' are, like me, part of a movement to develop a Spiritual Crisis Network, and the last, also like me, is now working in mental health. Unlike me, all have experienced the full force of the transliminal. All have managed to cope with these experiences, and ultimately to use them productively in their life's journeys.

CHAPTER 7

Travellers Across the Threshold

Without more ado, I will let Annabel tell you her story:

I am able to write positively about my journey because I have reached a place of deep healing in my present life. Had the outcome been different I may not have been a contributor to this book.

Mental health disturbance began in my mid teens with episodes of deep depression which required medication, and when 28 years old I experienced my first full blown psychotic episode. This coincided with my arrival in India in 1994, suggesting culture shock may have been one of the triggers.

For a number of years before going to India I knew I had to go; no reason, but instead a deep inner knowing. I first went to India in 1991 with my sister at a time when I was in a dark depressed state. I would happily not have gone but my sister's understandable insistence that I go as we had planned pushed me against my better judgement. I was unable to be in India for more than two days, and returned alone. On this return journey I met my host for my second and more positive trip to India. He was in the company of a Sadhu (Holy Man) who was going to the UK to meet his devotees, and for whom he was the translator. He voiced to me on our first meeting that he would show me the Real India. I visited this Sadhu several times, during my stay four years later, and I also travelled through India visiting sacred sites with the Hindu family I was staying with.

On my second trip, I stayed with this Hindu family in Northern India, and was the only western person in the household. One evening a spontaneous occurrence of unusually deep breathing led me into an altered state of consciousness which became so heightened that I had an ecstatic experience.

It was the spontaneous deep breathing that initiated the unfolding into ecstasy state, but there were stages in between. At first, I entered a space of deep grief in which I was unable to stop crying, and I intuited that I was connecting into the grief of the earth. This transformed into a much lighter mood, and I began laughing, and sensed I was pregnant and about to give birth. My body was getting increasingly hot and I had an urge to drink a lot of water. My hosts took me along to my bedroom and as I lay down, I experienced a golden light pouring into the crown of my head and with it the invitation to dream up a New Earth. Lots of thoughts came which had a strong theme of love, co-operation, creativity, respect for nature. Although my hosts were close to me it felt very important that they did not disturb me at this moment. When the process finished, I had a strange sensation in my hands as if they were growing flowers, and then my lower arms lifted up and then I made a very strong 'Ahhh' sound which was later remarked on as being very beautiful.

Not long after I went out into the courtyard garden which was in darkness, and where I lay down. As I lay, I heard music which arose from within my being, though seemed to be coming from the outside. It was so exquisite that it filled my body with a profound ecstasy in which every muscle in my face twitched with an unearthly delight and my body melted in a sweet surrender. I recall hearing choirs singing and also organ music.

After this elevated, unified state a much more fragmented

and dark phase took place. The threat of a nuclear attack became strong and although frightening I felt I could prevent its devastation. I recall seeing a snatch of TV in which a woman voiced 'They have dropped the bomb' which was weird and synchronous. Accompanying this experience was the sense of the earth going through a deep purification with seas going wild and winds raging. My sense was the clearing away of an old order so a new one might be born.

I also recall quietly reciting spell-like mantras to ward off what I perceived as negative influences. Another theme to enter me was The Holocaust which, like the threat of nuclear war, brought up much fear. Despite the fear element, I felt the captain of my own ship throughout the darker experiences. On a different note, there was a thread involving a reconnection with a past love and the promise of this reunion was a major element in my stamina for the process. I was so looking forward to the wedding feast that would take place when we found each other again.

On a physical level I was quite active, not sleeping much for two to three days. Awareness of my hosts' presence was generally limited. I recall one occasion when the grandmother and head of the household, Mama, was sitting close to my head as I lay. On leaning my head back I saw her face transform into that of an owl with laser-like beams coming from her eyes and into mine.

On the whole the relationship between me and my hosts was co-operative and peaceable, though on an occasion when I became less than calm they tried to limit my movements, and I recall ripping off my clothes so they could not use them to constrain me. The urge not to be controlled by anyone other than myself was powerful and I had the sense that my freedom had been curtailed in the distant past. I recall having a strong desire to get rid of my passport, reflecting that the whole world was my home and the notion of a passport was absurd.

Although much of the process was internal and invisible to others there were episodes in which my outward behaviour was clearly bizarre. My hosting family, whose spiritual roots were deep, instinctively trusted the process and though alarmed by my behaviour, kept me at home under close and loving watch. I had only one visit to a psychiatrist in which I was given two doses of anti-psychotic medication. What could be described as the acutely psychotic phase only lasted two to three days. The main treatment avenue was one of gentle nourishment, which included wholesome food, plentiful rest and regular Indian head massages. I recovered quickly and was able to spend a further nine months with this family enjoying India. I was left with a sense of unsolved mystery after this first experience of psychosis, which had not yet been tarnished by the brush of pathology.

However, it was not helpful that my host in India kept voicing that I had a special mission to perform on the earth. This message wove in and out of the whole India experience and I always felt uncomfortable about it.'

This rich account introduces many features of transliminal experience which I will pick up later, and I hope that it is clear from reading it that it mingles profound spiritual experience and what would ordinarily be labelled as psychosis (indeed Annabel so labels it) . Annabel's later experiences with the NHS mental health services when similar experiences recurred in England will follow, but next, I want to introduce Catherine's account of a parallel area of experience. Interestingly, where Annabel's took place in India, Catherine had her first encounter in Egypt.

Catherine' s Experience.

In April 2003 I found myself travelling back to the UK from Egypt in a wheelchair. I had been through an experience of spiritual emergency which was so extreme, so overwhelming emotionally, psychologically and spiritually, that my body had gone into shock. My legs had given way and I had not even been able to get from my hotel bed to the toilet.

During my brief stay in Egypt, at one point I experienced what felt like the entire suffering of humanity going back over thousands of years. The archetypal image that came to me was that of Avalokiteshvara, the Buddhist Bodhisattva figure who wept for the sorrow of mankind and who has a thousand arms to help relieve all the suffering. Another manifestation of perhaps the same compassionate, loving energy was that of the Divine Mother, whose gentle presence I felt very strongly within me.

I also experienced our natural state of inner peace, of a spaciousness that has no physical boundaries. It happened like this. One morning I was standing by the edge of the Nile, looking out over the vast expanse of this huge, majestic river. The sun was dancing on the ripples of the water's surface, bouncing off ... rays of glorious light falling and splashing off, almost like rain drops. As I watched individual light ray after light ray, falling, hitting the tiny crest of a ripple and bouncing back off, I moved into a meditative state. Mesmerised by the beauty of it, the simplicity and the repetitiveness of it, I fell into something of a trance like state. And then it happened. It was not the first time that sun dancing on the surface of water had had this effect on me, but this time it was much, much more powerful. I felt the boundaries of myself falling away. I looked over to the far bank, a very long way away, and realised that I had expanded, that I stretched as far as the bank and way up into the sky. I had become one with my surroundings. There was no solid me, only this beautiful, awesome feeling of expansiveness. And I knew this to be true. This is the truth of who I am. And I felt totally at peace. I felt the grace of love, of bliss.

We may tend to imagine that moving into a spacious boundless sense of being can be very blissful. And it can, but it can also be very frightening, because it is so unknown and new. It requires the breaking down of the self, which can be excruciating. There was an almighty inner battle, which had the profound physical effects I mentioned at the start of this account.

Another Word about Words.

As with Annabel's account, I will discuss the detailed learning from this glimpse into a transliminal experience in the next chapter, but will here note the term Catherine uses to describe her experience, 'spiritual emergency'. The strong similarities between the two experiences should be self evident, so this term appears to be another descriptor for the same thing. The term 'spiritual emergency' was coined by Stanislav Grof, whose therapeutic work and writings in this field are justly influential, and to whom I owe a considerable debt in clarifying the subject. However, 'spiritual emergency' carries with it a lot of assumptions, so I am going to avoid the term in my own exposition.

'Psychosis' is another term that carries many assumptions: assumptions that this experience is an illness; that the person should be under a psychiatrist and taking powerful medication in order to shut down this type of experience. The assumption behind 'spiritual emergency' is a bit more complex. Its companion term is 'spiritual emergence' - a process of spiritual growth towards enlightenment, which can take a turn for the dark and uncontrollable, hence the 'emergency'. This usage implies that it is possible to distinguish this process cleanly from a 'mere' psychosis. Therefore, though I have sympathy with the idea of accessing the transliminal as part of the journey of life, I avoid adopting this terminology.

It is time to turn to the darker part of the journey in the examples that follow.

Journey into the Dark

I am not sentimental about psychosis. I have worked in the mental health system for 15 years with people with severe and chronic problems. I know that encounters with the transliminal can have dire outcomes and blight people's lives. However, I do not think that this outcome is always predictable from the outset. In many (but not all) cases, it can go either way. Which way it goes will depend on a number of factors. One is undoubtedly the strength of the individual to withstand the onslaught of a full transliminal experience without fragmenting. Annabel and Catherine are both strong individuals! Context is another. Annabel's account gives a clear picture of the affirming and nurturing context within which her encounter took place. Catherine was also following a spiritual path and under spiritual guidance. These factors will have been vital in ensuring a benevolent outcome in the end.

On the other hand, it is clear from Annabel's account that she was behaving in ways that were sometimes alarming and sometimes bizarre. Her hosts must have had a strong nerve at times. In her second instalment she recounts what happened when similar events occurred in England. The course of the episode here was very different. Over to Annabel again.

Encounters with the Psychiatric Services.

One and a half years later, in 1996, back in the UK and employed as a nurse in a hospice, was the onset of my second experience of psychosis. This time I was not around people who could witness and hold the process and was instead sucked into the mental health system, under a section of the Mental Health Act (i.e., involuntarily detained) because no other approach was available at that time. I refused to leave my house voluntarily and because of my strength of resistance they used a strait jacket to get me into the ambulance.

It was terrifying, as well as humiliating to be pinned down

by a team of nurses and to be injected in the buttocks against my will on my arrival into a London psychiatric unit. Any time I showed excitability and refused medication led to forced injections and I invariably fell into a deep sleep from which I did not wake refreshed but despondent as to where I found myself. The physical environment was without warmth or softness, and the only regular human support was from other sufferers, whilst in the main the staff were an aloof presence. Clearly a profoundly different scenario to what took place when in India.

On discharge, 6 weeks later, I was not the confident, able, woman I had been two or three months before, and although my hospice job was kept open, I decided to resign from my post. Following 6 months recovery time, and a year working in temporary jobs, I moved to Worcestershire and began a nursing job in an Anthroposophical clinic

In 1998, I had my third experience of psychosis in which I was again involuntarily detained (in the UK). Although modern and relatively luxurious, the psychiatric unit still offered a predominantly medical approach, including forced injections and solitary confinement.

My fourth psychosis and final involuntary detention UK experience occurred in 2000, and on this occasion, handcuffs were used on my journey to the hospital in a police car. The inpatient stay echoed many of the unsavoury experiences of the other hospitalisations. On a positive note, there were always individual psychiatrists and staff members who made a positive impact through the wisdom and compassion they displayed, and I am very grateful to their presence. I have also had several Community Psychiatric Nurses over the years who have seen me on discharge, and who have been much appreciated. What has been lacking overall has been a deeper understanding of the process of psychosis, and as a result hospitalization experiences tend to compound misery rather than act as a kindly containment.

After the third and final hospitalization, I decided to take Carbomazapine regularly which I had hitherto resisted and continued with this for three to four years, before making an independent decision to bring the dose gradually to zero. I have not taken any medication for the last two and a half years with no ill effect.

I was highly fortunate to have enlightened employers between 1997 and 2002 who facilitated my re-entry into the work place after each of two hospitalizations, with a well thought through programme of support. This deeply affirming action was a significant aid to my recovery process. In many ways, I have been very fortunate although the trauma experienced during hospitalization under section of the Mental Health Act cannot be underestimated.

One of the major differences between the experience of psychosis in India as compared to the UK was that, after the hospitalizations in England I felt I had an incurable condition that would haunt me for the rest of my life and for which I would have to take life-long medication. This picture is powerful and disabling, and from personal experience, turns out not to be true.

Over the last five years I have been on a committed journey towards self healing which has addressed issues from childhood and facilitated a deepening relationship with my own body and spirit, and which is an ongoing process. I have visited a wide range of healers working on both physical and spiritual levels in addition to my own daily work of journaling, dream recording and also meditation. My life is rich on all fronts, and forever unfolding into new landscapes, and though frequently challenging. I have never felt as alive as I do today.'

I have included Annabel's account of the rest of her journey through the mental health system in full, as, though it ranges more widely than the strict argument of this section, it gives such a vivid picture of what does tend to happen in our country today to journeyers in the transliminal.

Psychosis from the Inside.

I am now going to introduce Matthew's account. Matthew manages brilliantly to convey the experience that led to his hospitalization, over 10 years ago now, from the inside. Matthew has since trained in the Buddhist discipline of Soto Zen. This has given him the groundedness needed to pursue both his spiritual life and his career without the distraction of these sorts of experiences. His spiritual tradition sees them as essentially a distraction from the true spiritual path, which is one of balance.

College Level exams.

A College student about 17-18 years old, I had been studying the philosophy of religion, and searching for God/Truth/Reality - I wanted to know and understand.

Finally - a 'breakthrough':

None of this is real; this life and universe is a great illusion. Fear of death is simply fear of letting this illusion go. The answer lies in surrender of this life - this reality... but how to wake up from this dream of life and death – how to reach; and see the face of God?

My friend had died age 16 two years before; he had been chased by drug dealers from a different part of town, He tried an escape along an electric train track, but slipped, was electrocuted and finished by a moving train. At last I could see: his death was a sign – he was a messenger calling into the unknown... He was guiding me out of this illusion

But how to escape? Great feelings started to come upon me as I reached beyond the world of illusion towards God. On Sunday I went to the village church where I was given another clue – "Welcome to the Arc" said a faithful villager. Yes THIS is the Arc, and only the presence of God can save us from the drowning world of illusion. ALL must wake up as I was waking up; or they would drown into the burning lake of sulphur.

Death

As the end of the 'illusion world' drew closer, Angels and Demons began to reveal themselves. The Angels were as a light leading to God, but the demons were as chains to the falsehood of illusion.

All around both Angels and evil forces of illusion became stronger. It was a battle of forces, but reassurances were given – that good would ultimately win.

At the bus stop on my way home from college I met angels who gave advice for my journey. They gave hints about the way ahead and the battles which must be fought. They told me what was in store. I returned to my village and met friends who were also angels. I tried to get them to DRINK THE WATER – to drink would ensure that they too would be saved from this evil world illusion and the burning lake of sulphur - they took some water; thus I knew they were safe.

We watched 'The Who' on a music video. The band on the video spoke directly to me; they too were angels and gave instructions. "It's beyond the beyond" an Angel (Pete Townsend) reassured as I struggled to reach beyond this world of illusion.

On my way home from my friend's house I searched for the vicar, to explain that the time as recorded in the Book of Revelation had come, but I could not find the vicar. I met a Minister and gave him the message: 'THE ONLY WORD WHICH CANNOT BE SAID IS THE WORD THIS IS TRYING TO SAY- SAY THE WORD'.

When I returned to my room at home with my parents I

needed to protect myself. I stayed in my room and created a 'circle' of safety. Demonic forces would try to attack me in the night. So, to remain in my circle of safety I prepared an empty container to urinate in. My drawings of patterns and designs which seemed to come from a divine source became protective, so I drew patterns on my clothes and college bag. These drawings were also a map showing the way I had to go...

As protection, to ward off the demonic forces I used my drum which was my most powerful weapon. It gave additional protective powers and it too was now covered in my patters and designs.

As I now sat protected in my room, I could hear more voices and discussion down stairs – it was demons in the guise of police, doctors, the vicar and others... Demons clearly seemed to be preparing for this battle too... Below and down the stairs was the underworld where I soon had to go. Demons had gathered their forces in preparation for battle, as I had prepared myself...

Hampshire County Lunatic Asylum

(Established under Provisions of Pauper Lunatics Act 1848 and the first patients were admitted in 1852. It was later known as Knowle Mental Hospital, Fareham and was closed in 1996).

When I opened my eyes again there were two people sat in front of me. There were windows but they had grids over them. There were other beds around but they were empty. There was a cupboard and I managed to grab a jug and turned it upside down so as to use it as a makeshift drum...

I sat for some time drumming to ward off any demonic attacks. But one of them complained that I was 'keeping other patients awake'- The demons were trying to break through my defence. Eventually a demon managed to snatch the jug away from me, and without a drum for protection I had lost an essential defence against impeding demonic attack.

Blood

Walking around the area of a few hospital beds, I saw a picture on the wall. It was a landscape painting. I looked at the picture for a long time. Eventually I realised that it was in fact a window into heaven – the reality beyond the illusion. In order to get there I had to 'show my faith'. I needed to allow my body to fall back in trust; by doing so I would more fully transcend the illusion and would land in heaven.

I fell back, but as I fell, BANG my head smacked onto the edge of a table. After a few moments I was able to stand – "that feels better" I said: The physical pain had created a brief but blissful momentary relief from mental torment. My head was now cut open and bled for quite a while.

Later I was asked if I wanted stitches in my head. But this was simply demons attempting to ensnare me in illusion –

"look at all the blood" they said.

"What blood?" I replied, "I can't see any blood" – The illusory blood coming out of my head was as a demonic chain - they tried to use it to control and ensnare me.

Force

A nurse had been walking behind me so as to assure I would not fall back again. After a while longer a team of people came into the area. I was pinned down by a team onto a bed and a needle was prepared to inject me by force.

Luckily the injection did nothing, I was able to get up and walk about and shouted at the nurses/demons surrounding me GO AWAY, GO AWAY, GO AWAY, GO AWAY, GO AWAY... I shouted for as long as I possibly could but was never violent in return for their needles.

Injected around 3-4 more times in this way, it had become a battle against their needle. The real control over me was that of demons. Some of those surrounding me would momentarily appear as angels but then turn into demons. They had a telephone they used to speak to the Doctor, they needed more drugs to keep me under control – it was simply an attempt to strengthen their demonic forces. Before they could make the call I smashed up the telephone. They also had radio communication, but in a moment of their distraction I grabbed and destroyed their Radio too.

More needles were brought in and this time the injection knocked me out and although I lay on the bed I could hear the people around talking about me – "he's a real nutter, this one".

Padded Cell

Later I was taken into a padded white room with a mattress on the floor and a radiator with especially curved edges. There was a window with a few bars on it and a round light on the ceiling.

A few would come to remove my soiled clothes. I physically resisted and fought against their demonic intrusions. I was held, sitting on the mattress for many hours, looking up to the small window with bars high on the wall.

Over the days demons continued to attack. In the evening demons appeared as my visiting parents. I was pleased to see them but this too was a demonic trap and deception. The arrival of these demons disguised as my parents meant I had to fight even harder to protect myself from their attempts at possession.

In the absence of a protective drum, I had begun chanting to protect myself. The repetitive sound of my chant created a protective circle around me. For hours and hours the chanting continued.

When demons appeared again as my parents, I had to once more prove that I had faith beyond the illusion of appearances. I knew that these were not my parents but demonic impersonators – everything around me remained an illusion and my battle within it was also my journey through it. I once again stood up ready to let myself fall back in full trust as I had before. This time a nurse caught my head before it hit the radiator.

Return

For many hours I continued to chant. Gradually I noticed that those around me became calmer, as did I. As all became more and more settled, the demons were more pacified - chant induced pacification gradually overpowered the demonic forces. Still in my padded cell, I looked up at the small round light above the mattress and lay back. Just as I had entered the underworld via the staircase at home, as I looked into the small round light above me, I could now see the exit out of the underworld, and it was time to leave. I looked at the light for as long as I could, and fell into a natural sleep...

When I awoke, I said "Thank God that's over", the demons were now pacified – the depths of psychosis confronted and travelled through, thus the world, at least for me, was indeed fresh and new. I told the person who had been sitting on a chair outside all night watching me that it was over, I was back and wanted something to eat. He asked me to take some medication – Droperidol, a drug which is now deemed too unsafe for medical use. A few weeks later I was back at college continuing with my 'A' Levels, and had stopped taking any medication whatsoever.

With the help of Matthew, we have moved from experiences which are identifiably spiritual to those that are identifiably psychotic - and we can see the situation both from Matthew's point of view at the time, and from the viewpoint of those charged with looking after him and dealing with his behaviour. It is time to move on to look at the features and logic of the transliminal that can be drawn from these accounts.

CHAPTER 8

Making Sense of the Transliminal

So what have these strange and at times frankly mad experiences to do with ordinary spirituality, normal religion and the survival of God in a secular age? The key, I would argue, is the transliminal - that experience beyond the threshold which most of us glimpse but which the adventurers of the previous two chapter encountered in its full and terrifying force. Few are completely immune to the attractions of the transliminal, which entice through promise of mystery and the radically unsolvable riddles of human existence. The myths of the third chapter point to such riddles. However, it is only the intrepid or the foolhardy that enter the transliminal hook line and sinker. Of these, some emerge deeper and wiser; others lose their way, and their sense of self fragments. This madness can be temporary and surmountable, as we have seen in the last chapter. For others it is tragically a lifelong state.

Another puzzle is why some people, like Annabel and Catherine trip across the threshold spontaneously, whereas the closest most of us get is a breathtaking sunset or self transcending sex. (Of course, a form of the experience is also purchasable from the drug dealer...) Achieving a stilling of the self through religious/spiritual practice such as meditation or prayer is hard work for people like me. The experiences of St. Teresa, St. John of the Cross, Julian of Norwich and the others came about in the context of disciplined devotion to the contemplative life. It was in a context of Buddhist practice that Catherine embarked on her journey; Annabel's second trip to India was involved with spiritual seeking through the connection with the Sadhu. For Matthew, disciplined spiritual practice enabled him to harness his tendency to openness to the transliminal in safe and productive ways in his subsequent life, and Annabel too has found more regular meditation helpful. All these individuals just found themselves in that other dimension Most of us never find the doorway. Why is it almost too accessible for some and hard of access for most of the rest of us?

Measuring Difference.

The eminent psychological researcher, Gordon Claridge, can help us here. Claridge's work follows in the tradition of the great Hans Eysenck who explored the individual differences in temperament through giving people questionnaires to complete in the 1960s and '70s. Eysenck was researching the notion that these differences, in introversion, extraversion and neuroticism for instance, were grounded in physical differences between people in their 'arousability' - that is their reactions, in particular their stress reaction. Since the human arousal mechanism is mediated by chemical messengers in the nervous system, the idea that this variability is at bottom physical makes a lot of sense. Eysenck's work in devising personality questionnaires to distinguish the different types is the basis for all those personality tests that Human Resources departments use when interviewing people for jobs.

Claridge was also measuring human difference, based on physical differences between people, and using questionnaires. The difference between people that he was interested in was openness or otherwise to unusual experiences - in other words, openness to the transliminal (his word, via Thalbourne, remember!) He called this Schizotypy. In the same way that Eysenck's questionnaires gave people a score for neuroticism, so that you (or your potential employer) could tell whether you were more or less neurotic than most other people, Claridge's questionnaires sorted people out according to where they lay on the schizotypy spectrum. If you scored highly, you were a high schizotype – you had more of it than other people; if you scored at the other end, you had less of it.

The word schizotypy is a bit forbidding because of its associations with the dreaded 'schizophrenia', and obtaining a high schizotypy score on one of Claridge's questionnaires does indeed predict greater vulnerability to psychotic breakdown. However, schizotypy research (which is something of an industry) has identified a lot of other associations. High schizotypes are more likely to be highly creative; the artists and visionaries of their generation. They are also those with the most attuned spiritual sense - those most open to spiritual experience. My confidence that there is a real overlap and confusion between spirituality and psychosis is built on the solid foundation of research undertaken by ex-students of Claridge such as Mike Jackson. Jackson's carefully researched PhD thesis, which has been built upon by the research of his students and collaborators, establishes this link very powerfully.

Evidence of Overlap

Mike Jackson's research combined quantitative (large scale questionnaire) and qualitative (detailed analysis of a few in depth interviews) methods of investigation. He first screened a large population for transliminal experiences. He needed to devise a whole classification system for such experiences especially for this study. He then compared the group with the highest rating on such experiences with a sample of people under the mental health services, who had acquired a diagnosis of psychosis. In common with a number of similar studies, this revealed strong overlap between the types of experience reported by the two groups. The differences were partly in degree of distress and disturbance occasioned by their experiences, and interestingly, in the nature of their social and/or spiritual context. Where they had a benign way of making sense of what was happening to them, that did not undermine their self esteem (in the way that a diagnosis of schizophrenia tends to), they were far less likely to be distressed, and to find their life disrupted. Consequently, they did not feel the need to seek help from the psychiatric services.

The qualitative study went further into this fascinating area of overlap by interviewing an equal number of individuals on either side of the divide. The resulting accounts underline the impossibility of drawing hard and fast lines between spiritual experiences and those that come to the attention of the mental health system. My edited book on psychosis and spirituality, listed at the end, contains chapters by both Gordon Claridge and Mike Jackson which cover their research in much more detail.

The schizotypy spectrum

To return to the schizotypy spectrum, we all lie somewhere on this spectrum. The high schizotypes are those, like Annabel, Catherine and Matthew, who are liable to trip into that other dimension of transliminality without too much warning. They are also, frequently, the sensitive and creative people. Indeed, harnessing their spirituality in a grounded way, or developing their creative expression, whether through art or action in the world, can be the way to ensure that their transliminal journeying leads to growth, flourishing and transformation as opposed to sinking into persisting (as opposed to transient) madness. Annabel, Catherine and Matthew all illustrate this positive use of their gift in different ways.

I would argue that all of us have some measure of openness to this other way of experiencing, however limited. It is that which is most vital; most precious for us. How it is encountered; how it is expressed varies enormously between individuals and cultures. Traditionally, communal religious practice was the vehicle for this expression. In our more individualistic age, what was once a universal habit of communal worship has become optional, but we have let the transliminal into our lives in other ways; it is hard to keep out!

The experiences of the previous two chapters can help illuminate the concept of the schizotypy spectrum. They also illustrate the features and regularities of transliminal experience in its extreme form. This should help us to recognise it in the more watered down version that most of us will meet in our daily lives. In what follows, I will draw out particular features of the transliminal that are illustrated by the journeys taken by Annabel, Catherine and Matthew.

Loss of Boundaries.

The first thing to happen to both Annabel and Catherine in their ecstatic encounters was a stepping out of their individual selves and experiencing themselves as part of the universe. As Catherine says: "There was no solid me, only this beautiful, awesome feeling of expansiveness." There are two important aspects to this experience; firstly, what happens to the ordinary sense of self, and secondly, the experience of loss of boundaries. The loss of boundaries and distinctions crops up at other points in these accounts. For instance, Matthew confuses angels and demons - figments of his fevered imagination - with real people such as his friends and the hospital staff, and, as in this example, even his parents: "In the evening demons appeared as my visiting parents. I was pleased to see them but this too was deception. The arrival of these demons disguised as my parents meant I had to fight even harder to protect myself from their attempts at possession." In another example common amongst people in hospital, Annabel experiences the TV speaking to her innermost concerns: "I recall seeing a snatch of TV in which a woman voiced 'They have dropped the bomb' which was weird and synchronous." These examples illustrate the boundary between the inner and outer worlds breaking down.

Sense of Mission

All three journeyers experience a sense of mission, which in the
case of the first two alternates with a loss of self. Annabel sees
herself involved in a renewal of the earth, and this aspect is
suggested where Catherine says: "Another manifestation of
perhaps the same compassionate, loving energy was that of the
Divine Mother, whose gentle presence I felt very strongly within
me." Matthew was consumed by a mission to ward off the
demons. Annabel's account shows most clearly the temptation to
read this aspect of the experience as a sign of specialness or
divinity. She states that this was her host's interpretation which
she found distinctly unhelpful. It is a tribute to her groundedness
that she was able to appreciate a crucial truth about the
transliminal, and so resist this temptation.

Beyond boundaries logic changes, as discussed earlier, when
the idea of 'both-and' logic was introduced. Things are no longer
this or that; either black or white; either god or human being.
Entering the transliminal, you leave these distinctions and
categories behind, and so find yourself in a world of 'both - and' -
two contradictory things can be absolutely and authentically true
at the same time. You can be both god and human being. So can
everybody else! I will return again to the problems that arise when
people get the logic of the two states mixed up. Julian of
Norwich's vision of the world, simultaneously as small as a
hazelnut and embracing the whole, is a nice example of managing
to hold both ends of the paradox at a time.

The Logic of the Transliminal.

I have argued earlier that the transliminal and the unconscious are
approximately different words for the same thing, but with
different associations. If we turn again to the psychoanalytic literature, we also find a recognition that the unconscious works on a
different logic. Freud identified this sort of thinking as 'primary
process' thinking. These ideas have been developed furthest by

the psychoanalytic writer, Matte Blanco, who has a small but dedicated following. Matte Blanco calls the logic of the unconscious 'Symmetric Logic', as opposed to ordinary logic, which is by contrast, 'Asymmetric Logic'. I will let a contemporary exponent of Matte Blanco's ideas, Rodney Bomford, explain. (Bomford has written accessibly about the somewhat inaccessible Matte Blanco).

> Symmetric logic is the invention, or discovery of Ignacio Matte Blanco (1913-95) a psycho-analyst in the Freudian and Kleinian traditions who had also a strong amateur interest in mathematics and in philosophy. Symmetric logic enabled him to discern patterns in the thinking of schizophrenic patients which accounted for assertions and deductions made by them which the ordinary person would regard as nonsensical madness. As he reflected further on this logic, Matte Blanco saw that it provided a wider, more generalised theory that explained the characteristics of unconscious thinking as Freud had formulated them long before. Since feeling and emotion are held by psycho-analytic theory to be the result of unconscious process, symmetric logic sheds light on how emotion affects thinking, on how, therefore, each of us sees the world and responds to events concerning us. Our minds are not purely rational but intimately combine rational, logical thought with all manner of matters of feeling and emotion which are often called simply irrational. Matte Blanco used symmetric logic to show that the irrational has deep patterns of thought and is not therefore, as might otherwise be assumed, wholly random and erratic. (from Bomford's chapter on Matte Blanco and the Logic of God in the book "Ways of Knowing" edited by Chris Clarke - yes there is a connection!)

A different quality of experience – introducing 'the numinous'.

As well as its singular logic, there are other features of the transliminal that are well illustrated by the accounts in the two preceding chapters. The quality of the experience feels different. It feels important. The German theologian, Rudolf Otto, struggled to pin down this quality in his book: 'The Idea of the Holy', back in 1917. He coined the word 'numen' or 'numinous' to describe it, as he noted that all the usual terms had unhelpful associations that made them inadequate to capture what he was after. The term 'Holy' had become synonymous with 'good' which was far too limiting. Other commentators had noted the human responses of extreme humility in the presence of deity, and the reckless compassion we have already identified, but he felt that something was missing. Otto identified the missing element as 'mysterium tremendum' and described this challenging concept as follows:

> The feeling of ('mysterium tremendum') may at times come sweeping like a gentle tide, pervading the mind with a tranquil mood of deepest worship. It may pass over into a more set and lasting attitude of the soul, continuing, as it were, thrillingly vibrant and resonant, until at last it dies away and the soul resumes its 'profane', non-religious mood of everyday experience. It may burst in sudden eruption up from the depths of the soul with spasms and convulsions, or lead to the strangest excitements, to intoxicated frenzy, to transport, and to ecstasy. It has its wild and demonic forms and can sink to an almost grisly horror and shuddering. It has its crude, barbaric antecedents and early manifestations, and again it may be developed into something beautiful and pure and glorious. It may become the hushed, trembling, and speechless humility of the creature in the presence of – whom or what? In the presence of that which is a *Mystery* inexpressible and above all creatures.

I have quoted this passage at length, as it does seem to cover the range, both of the accounts in the last chapter and of the experiences of Julian, Teresa and John in the one before. Otto captures well that sense of crossing a threshold from the everyday, and in particular nails that sense of 'holy awe' or 'the fear of God' which has been much misunderstood. When humans encounter angels in the Christian bible, the first words of the angel are usually something like: 'Fear not'. In other words the recipient is being instructed to pick themselves up off the floor, where they had flung themselves in terror, so that the divine messenger can usefully deliver his message. This gives us some idea of the impact of the encounter. Too often, the fear of God is represented as fear of God's judgement, of eternal damnation. As the automatic response to the angel and the passage from Otto make clear, it is something far more fundamental and immediate than that – and something far more significant.

The concept of the 'numinous' has gained wider currency because it was taken up by Jung. To sum up: we can identify the numinous by a strong sense of the supernatural; we are in a different country; we have accessed a different dimension. There are no guarantees about what it is going to be like in this dimension. It could be blissful and peaceful, or it could be terrifying. The adventurer has crossed the threshold of certainty.

A Sense of Conviction

Paradoxically, along with this experience of numinosity goes a sense of absolute certainty. This sense of certainty can represent the benevolent destiny of the guardian angel – falling in love with the right person, for example. However, it can equally well be tricksterish and unreliable. 'Both-and' again! This sort of absolute conviction of certainty led both Annabel and Matthew to resist external control vigorously. This 'delusional' (another word with a lot of baggage!) conviction is one of the complications of working therapeutically with, or indeed nursing, people experiencing episodes of madness.

Where does this different quality of experience come from? My answer, which will be backed up with more detail from cognitive science in the next chapter, is as follows. The loss of boundaries and categories that gives us symmetric logic suggests that the part of the mind that normally divides and categorizes has got switched off (temporarily) when we enter a transliminal state. As well as sorting things out, this part of our mind also filters our perceptions. When our minds are working in the ordinary way, what we see and experience is partly determined by what we expect to see and experience, based on the picture of the world laboriously constructed by our minds throughout our lives. Beyond this filter we encounter the whole. The experience is overwhelming - 'Mind blowing'. We are temporarily disconnected from the means to fit it into that picture of the world and reality that we normally rely on. In terms of Kelly's construct theory, we have moved beyond the constructs. This experience can be ecstatic and exhilarating. It can also be extremely frightening. The paradoxical experience of the Christian mystics quoted earlier; the dark cloud, or dark night of the soul that seemed inseparable from the loving union with God, can also be understood in this way.

Cosmic Suffering

Another striking similarity between the accounts of Annabel and Catherine is their sense of being overwhelmed with suffering. There is also a powerful parallel here with the visions of Julian, and other Christian mystics. This is not individual suffering, but cosmic suffering; the ills of the world assailed Annabel and Catherine, producing overwhelming sadness. In the case of Annabel this suffering conjured up The Holocaust. Fear was another overwhelming emotion, cited by both Annabel and Matthew. For Annabel, nuclear war was the image that this produced; Matthew experienced it as a struggle with all around him who had for him become demons in a cosmic adventure.

These examples illustrate two aspects of the transliminal. One is that emotion becomes vast and volatile when in this state – it switches and is cosmic in scope and intensity. The other is that that sense of sorrow and infinite compassion that is a marked feature of the accounts of Annabel and Catherine can lead to compassionate and responsible action in the world, once the traveller has emerged from their transliminal journey. This is usually expected of the mystic in the great faith traditions, and was illustrated by St. Teresa, St. John of the Cross, and Julian. This has happened in the case of all three of our examples. Among other involvements, Annabel and Catherine are deeply committed to providing better and more sensitive support to future transliminal travellers through the Spiritual Crisis Network, and Matthew has returned to the mental health services – to serve as a professional, but one who will bring a far richer understanding of his work than most.

I stated earlier that I consider a justice dimension to be the mark of an authentic spirituality or religion. Similarly, I would see justice action as the mark of a mature transliminal traveller. Those who merely revel in the experience or 'trip' (and possibly unkindly, I would put most of the people who access this experience through street drugs into that category) and bring nothing back into the shared world, and those who get lost in it through persisting insanity, have failed to complete the process in this way. Maybe they were unable to grasp and use the gift they were offered. Maybe they themselves were given insufficient help to complete their journey safely, or were in other ways trapped in the transliminal state.

Supernatural Entities.

As well as experiencing this sense of numinosity, two of our three travellers (Catherine and Matthew) also met supernatural entities on their journey. Catherine met Avalokiteshvara, and the Divine

Mother, in a merged form, and Matthew encountered angels and demons. Annabel too had a partially personified sense of the Earth. Catherine identifies her encounter with Jung's notion of the archetype. Archetypes are themes or figures of great power that are encountered in the transliminal. Jung was able to demonstrate that the same archetypes recur throughout both time and space, cropping up in mythologies and peoples' dreams from earliest times to the present. He called them 'Symbols of Transformation' (the title of one of his books) because of their potential to aid the work of integration of the individual. However, like all aspects of the transliminal, they also had the potential to be destructive and dangerous.

There is thus recognition that as well as symmetric logic, the unconscious or transliminal is a place of supernatural beings, or a place where natural beings become supernatural, like 'Mama' in Annabel's account, who appeared as an owl with laser eyes, and Matthew's parents.

The sheer power of these supernatural beings or archetypes, whether terrifying, benevolent or both assail the traveller. In a place of no boundaries, they threaten to take over, devour, inhabit or become the journeyer. The distinction between inner and outer has dissolved here, so who knows whether they arise from deep within or invade from outside. Such concepts have no meaning in this place. That is why Jung referred to the 'collective uncon- scious'. The boundaries between minds; between people do not exist here. The transliminal is shared territory.

In his writings, Jung gives countless examples where people with no knowledge of the relevant mythologies describe characters from the legends of distant cultures. Equally, the identification of these demonic/angelic beings can often be traced to the culture of the experiencer. Catherine knew a thing or two about Bodhisattvas; Annabel was concerned for the plight of the earth. People in hospital with psychotic episodes today complain of rays beamed into their brains from space ships, where a few centuries ago, the same encounters would have been labelled as invading spirits. I keep an open mind about invading entities and the like, and hold several, doubtless incompatible, possibilities simultaneously. We are here in the realm of mystery, beyond precise knowledge.

The Physical Dimension – Risk.

A final observation from these transliminal experiences; despite being essentially private and interior - Annabel specifically tracks how distant she was from her un-intrusive but containing hosts - there was a physical side to these episodes. Both Annabel and Matthew attempted to resist control, and both suffered restraint and involuntary medication as a result (Annabel during her later episodes). It is possible to imagine how these episodes appeared to those on the outside, and where conflict and coercion became necessary. From my own perspective, I have deep sympathy for both those on the inside, and those on the outside with a responsibility to keep things safe. The coercive apparatus of the mental health system; for instance, the Mental Health Act under which people can be involuntarily detained in the UK, come about because of this potential for risk. The less respectable sections of the media have succeeded in stirring up panic about this risk by gross exaggeration of the proportion of assaults and homicides perpetrated by people under the influence of psychosis. This only adds to the climate of fear and control surrounding the subject of madness.

CHAPTER 9

Pathways in the Brain

Having labelled the phenomena described in the previous chapter as unknowable mystery, I am now going to attempt to apply my knowledge as a psychologist to explain what is going on. I am well into symmetric logic, where two incompatible things can coexist!

I have referred a number of times to the idea that there are two distinct cognitive systems: one governing logical, verbal knowledge and the other governing what can loosely be classified for now as 'the rest'. It is the existence of these two systems that gives us the two ways of knowing. I have also suggested that there is an evolutionary dimension to all this. The development of language and precise logical thought distinguishes us from our non-human ancestors, so that this new bit of apparatus was presumably bolted onto the standard- issue ape brain, which was well suited to survival, propagation, social relations, social hierarchy and all the rest. We still use that model for all these very essential functions. It is the fancy new, language, bit that has been bolted on. As everyone who has added an exciting new feature to an existing model knows, it can affect the smooth functioning of the original – adversely!

This common sense idea about evolution and the two systems in the brain is born out by detailed experimentation into the way cognition works. These experiments have examined aspects of memory, discovering among other things that memories coded in different modalities (i.e. verbally, visually etc.) are stored in different places. Experiments have explored every possibility of limitations in processing capacity, for instance, by getting people to do more things at once than they possibly can.

Two types of processing

Through a lot of detailed work, a picture of how the different bits of the brain work together has started to emerge. There is some controversy about how precisely to make sense of all this mind-numbingly detailed data. There is general agreement that the sort of processing we use to get out of the way of imminent danger (lorry bearing down; sabre toothed tiger poised for attack) is distinct from the sort of processing we use to solve mathematical problems or compose a piece of prose. I have adopted a particular cognitive model that goes further than the others in its power to explain, as this model, to my mind, supplies the answers to the riddle of the transliminal.

The model goes by the title of Interacting Cognitive Subsystems (ICS for short), and was first written up in detail by two psychologists, John Teasdale and Phillip Barnard in 1993, in a book called 'Affect, Cognition and Change'. Teasdale is a clinical psychologist like myself, as well as being an academic researcher, and he was particularly interested in explaining depression. Barnard is a pure academic with an amazing capacity to master detail. The computer graphics he employs to expound his theory of the architecture of cognition are mind boggling, and in detail, quite beyond me.

I am not alone in being daunted by the detailed exposition of the model. The whole theory has proved a bit too incomprehensible for a lot of people, but gradually, these exciting and ground breaking ideas about how the brain is organized are starting to sink in. As I read the current clinical psychology journals, I note with satisfaction that there are now frequently reported new bits of research based on this model. It is being cited in the latest books on Cognitive Behaviour Therapy as the most authoritative explanation of how our thinking works. My own work in developing effective therapies for people in crisis and with severe problems is grounded in this model. Evaluation of this approach has produced good results, which have been published and are arousing interest. So, without further ado, I will explain why ICS seems to me to hold the key to understanding the link between mystery, madness and the survival of God.

ICS is a model of cognitive architecture – how the pathways in the brain connect; which connects with which and which doesn't – using the data from the research base sketched in at the beginning of this chapter. It concludes that the different functions of the brain, like vision, movement, hearing, speech etc. all have their own distinct subsystems. Moreover, these minor subsystems are organized by two, over-arching subsystems at the top of a hierarchy.

The missing boss.

It is these two organizing subsystems that will concern us from now on. Both these two top systems are concerned with meaning – working out what is going on. However, they are very different in character and sphere of operation, because they connect with distinct groups of lower subsystems. That distribution is a bit uneven. One 'top' subsystem only gets direct information from the couple of subsystems that deal with speech and language. As the different subsystems pass the bits of information to each other using their own particular code or modality, these speech and language systems use exclusively verbal coding.

The other main subsystem gets all the rest, coded in a vivid assortment of sound, sight, smell, body movement and bodily arousal. The bodily arousal subsystem is the bit that governs stress, excitement, sleep etc. The verbal/logical organizing subsystem is called in ICS 'The Propositional', and from now on I will use that term. Teasdale and Barnard call their other main organizing subsystem 'The Implicational'. However, because its function is emotion, which is the human way of organizing relationship, I will call it 'The Relational'. I hope that the possible connection between Matte Blanco's symmetric logic and the relational subsystem has just struck you!

The brilliant feature of this model is that neither of these two is the boss and most of the time they work by smoothly communicating with each other and handing the baton of responsibility backwards and forwards. There is no boss. That means that you, and I and everyone, is a balancing act. The single self of our consciousness is an illusion. I think that that explains an awful lot about being human. It also fatally undermines the concept of the isolated, purely individual, billiard ball mind.

Explaining the Transliminal

Barnard has applied this model to psychosis. He has worked out (in excruciatingly fine detail) how the two main subsystems can become 'desynchronised'. This means that the two systems are no longer 'in synch' or working smoothly together, so that information gets lost. In the case of ICS, it is somehow always the propositional that gets left behind when this happens. Barnard tracks convincingly how this produces all the familiar symptoms of psychosis. In my terms this makes perfect sense, because the verbal, propositional, system produces precise, either-or, logic. When the relational is temporary stranded without the propositional, it does not have access to the means of making these precise distinctions. The person is left with all the rest, all the sensory information, but with no way of really finding their bearings. The propositional manages boundaries. In the relational there are no boundaries because the propositional limits and filters. Without this filter, everything acquires a supernatural, numinous, glow.

The relational is about emotion, relationship and the situation of the self. When the relational becomes decoupled from the propositional, all of these properties of emotion and relationality can overwhelm consciousness with a sense of cosmic significance, in often contradictory ways. The boundary between inner and outer dissolves along with the other boundaries, so that memories, thoughts, and who knows, - even outside influences - are experienced as voices. Unlike Barnard, I see all this applying to spiritual/ mystical experience as well as to obvious psychosis. (Barnard is not very interested in spirituality, but is tolerant of my interpretations of his theory!)

What makes this happen? As with the schizotypy classification discussed earlier, the arousal system, which is governed by chemicals in the nervous system, is crucial. This explains why chemicals, in the form of medication, are used by the mental health services to regulate the process. We all switch off our propositional subsystems and leave the relational in charge when we go to sleep – when our arousal is at its lowest. Dreams are the commonest sort of transliminal experience. So, very low arousal is a time when this sort of desynchrony can occur. However, high arousal; stressed states can also have exactly the same effect.

It is well recognized that psychotic breakdown often first occurs at stressful and disorienting times of life. Matthew's friend had just been killed, for instance, just before his breakdown. Julian of Norwich was suffering a near fatal illness when her visions came to her. It makes sense, after all, that the logical propositional should operate in conjunction with the relational in that alert, concentrated, state of mind in the middle, and give up if things either get too hectic, or if the propositional gets switched off when concentration drifts, or in sleep.

Mike Jackson, whose research into the overlap between psychotic and spiritual experience I have referred to, argues that psychosis, or a transliminal experience, can serve a problem solving function. Suppose life has come to a bit of a dead end for one reason or another then, if the individual is fairly high on the schizotypy spectrum, or is undertaking the right sort of spiritual or religious practices, or taking the right sort of substances, crossing into the transliminal can offer an escape into another dimension.

I have already noted that the transliminal is associated with creativity. This escape therefore has the potential to be a source of originality and new meanings, and can enable that individual to find an original way out of their dilemma. However, it also brings with it the danger of getting stuck on the wrong side of the threshold. Spending too long in a state where either-or logic is out of reach spells confusion, inability to function normally in the world, and so madness,

To return to the argument about different states of arousal and access to the transliminal, a little more explanation is needed. Most of us travel backwards and forwards between the desynchronized state of sleep and the synchronized one of waking without so much as a whisper of a strange experience, and those we have while sleeping, are safely discountable as dreams. Entering a fully transliminal state in the middle of waking life is clearly a bit different from that. However, moving between the dominance (or buffering, to use the technical term) of the propositional and the dominance of the relational within daily life is so much part of our experience that we do not think twice about it. I have already referred to the way in which our thinking processes are alternately buffered with one or other of the main meaning making systems in an earlier chapter, where I compared this process to flitting between two very different adjoining rooms in a house, but briefly pausing on the threshold of each.

While I concentrate on writing this text, my propositional is in charge. If I get a bit stuck; look out of the window; daydream in the hope that a good phrase will come to me – the relational has taken over but when the phrase comes, the propositional clicks in again. Normally the propositional and relational are just good partners and work so smoothly together that we do not notice what they are up to.

Then there is the attraction of having a bit of a holiday from the busy propositional. There are a whole host of ways of turning off the propositional, including religious practices such as chanting and fasting, and less religious practices (though this depends on which religion!) such as drugs and alcohol. For most, this is just a brief holiday, and the propositional is soon in business again. However, a fair proportion of the younger people who arrive in the hospital where I work with their first, or nearly their first, psychosis, have been taking drugs. Their friends were able to access the transliminal and return. They could not get back.

CHAPTER 10

A Neuron's Eye View and Facing the Critics

I am often asked: are the two main subsystems not just the left brain, right brain distinction? The answer is as follows. The neural systems I am talking about connect different centres of processing capacity, and it is absolutely true that the spatial processing capacity is predominantly sited in the right brain, the language capacity in the left. So far, they correspond nicely with the propositional and the relational. However, these two subsystems are about meaning making; making sense of the whole picture. They use processing capacity from many different parts of the brain and integrate it to do this, so the full answer is that the picture is more complicated.

Indeed, most of the excitement and headlines about the discovery of some scientific basis for spirituality, belief etc. concern neuroscience rather than cognitive organization. I can only agree that neuroscience seems much more cutting edge, much more riveting than memory experiments (in fact, it is difficult to find anything much duller than a standard issue memory experiment!) And then there is the recent development of those wonderful psychedelically coloured pictures produced by functional magnetic resonance imaging (fMRI). These show the blood flow in the brain. As the bits of the brain that are working are the ones that use blood, these images can reveal which bits of the brain are active at any given moment. Why I have I not followed suit? Most of the cognitive research that forms the bedrock of ICS was conducted in the 1970s and 1980s, whereas neuroscience is constantly coming up with new claims.

Once again, though, ICS is a theory of interconnections and networks within the brain, the connections are between different parts of the brain, and the broad picture we get from ICS is informed by our knowledge of the distinct functions of the different bits of the brain. ICS clarifies which different bits are in direct communication and which are not. The chemically and electrically controlled actions of our neurons make this communication possible. I will briefly look at what we know about these aspects next.

Which bit does what in the brain.

Long before the detail revealed by the MRI scan was available, it was known that particular parts of that squidgy mass of computational complexity we call the brain govern particular functions. Those who had the misfortune to suffer horrible, but neatly discrete, damage to their brains, without being killed by the event, were the first to advance this science. The effect on their personality and functioning could be noted and related to the site of the damage. Linking the location of strokes (caused by disruption of blood flow to a part of the brain that effectively switches it off) and other brain disease to the resulting disability also enables the neuroscientist to pinpoint which bit of grey matter governs which faculty; depending on whether speech or movement is affected, for instance, and in what way.

The other, well established, knowledge about the way the brain works concerns the details of chemically governed electrical activity that passes messages constantly back and forth between the various parts. These neuronal messages depend on a constant balance between excitation and inhibition, whether it is excitation or inhibition of a neuronal pathway that wins through at any particular moment will determine whether a particular stimulus results in action or conscious experience or not. Psycho-pharmacology has gone far in learning how to intervene in these processes through a bewildering array of psychoactive medications. However, they are still a relatively blunt instrument. The 'side effects' they inevitably produce demonstrate this, as their action impacts not only on the targeted neuronal activity, but on a lot of other things as well. Given the intricate complexity of these neuronal pathways of the brain, this is not surprising.

Linking this with ICS

So, how do the propositional and relational subsystems mesh with what we know about how the brain works? Obviously, the propositional will be mainly concerned with the language centres, such as the parietal lobe, and the sophisticated, multi-functional, frontal lobes. However, they will also need the hippocampus for memory, and probably a lot else besides. The amygdala, which governs raw emotion, will clearly feature in the interconnections that make up the relational subsystem – but so will almost every other part of the brain. Indeed, language in its emotional and poetic usages will also feature.

There are some details of brain functioning that complement the picture drawn by ICS. It has long been recognized that there is a fast track system for reacting to danger stimuli, governed by the amygdala, which bypasses conscious appraisal. This works through the release of stress hormones from the adrenal gland – the so called 'fight or flight' response. When this system comes into operation, the more complex processing capacities are inhibited. This is the mechanism whereby the arousal system governs the communication between the propositional and relational subsystems in ICS. The operation of the fight or flight response is understood in detail (see Joseph Ledoux's very readable book, 'The Emotional Brain' for a good description of this).

It is well understood that low arousal, and sleep is governed by the limbic system. The way in which high arousal (stress) as well as low arousal (sleep and daydreaming) leads to the propositional and relational parting company, so that the relational is left in charge, has been described earlier. The neuro-physiological mechanism for these crucial disconnections is therefore reasonably well understood.

Of course, the advent of the PET scan and other advanced technologies has made it possible to look at the functioning brain while it is working. People can be given tasks to perform, or be instructed to call up memories or have experiences induced. Because they have previously been given an injection of radioactive dye, or 'tracer', the part of the brain involved will light up in the scanner. It is this technology that has recently given us some more clues about what might be going on in the brain when someone is having a spiritual experience.

The 'God Spot' debate

I referred earlier to Steve Connor's claim to have located a 'God spot' in the brain, by discovering the site implicated in the mystical experiences that can sometimes precede the fit in temporal lobe epilepsy. This was later demonstrated by Michael Persinger, using a specially designed helmet to stimulate the relevant bit of brain. Persinger's experiment clearly showed that subjects who did not know what was likely to happen had somewhat spooky experiences, for instance, of 'a presence', from using the helmet. Whether they ascribed a religious meaning to this or not depended on whether they had a pre existing belief system or whether they hadn't. This can be seen as an example of the propositional coming up with an explanation after the event! The propositional can always be relied upon to be ready with an explanation; any explanation.

The debate that followed concerned whether or not these data had 'explained away' faith and religion or not. Once again, people tended to line up on one side or another according to whether they were dyed in the wool sceptics or had spiritual/religious sympathies! As I have already argued, I would expect any human experience to be linkable to corresponding brain activity. Where precisely in the brain that activity takes place does not seem to me to be overwhelmingly significant, but other people obviously find this aspect more exciting than I do. What I would contend is that finding the site in the brain, or otherwise proving the existence of brain activity, does not 'explain away' the experience. In the case of difficult to explain experiences like the one Persinger induced, they could sometimes come about because of particular neuronal activity, as in the case of experiences caused by the epilepsy, but could equally suggest greater responsiveness to a wider sphere of influence than people are usually open to – the sort of responsiveness that characterizes someone more open to the transliminal.

Other researchers have followed up on this work, and, predictably, the picture has become more complicated as a result. Particularly interesting are Dr. Andrew Newberg's findings using PET scanning techniques on Franciscan nuns and Tibetan Buddhists actually during prayer/meditation. His results showed that a number of different areas lit up on the scanner pictures when the subjects were in deep meditation. In particular he found that when his subjects reported a sense of unity, oneness with all, the part of the brain that governs the sense of individual agency, the parietal lobe, became inactive. This is compatible with the idea that when the relational subsystem takes over, the sense of being an individual self, which is bound up with the propositional, will take a back seat. Dr. Newberg was careful to stress that, whatever his findings did show, they did not disprove or otherwise the 'truth' of religion!

Mirror Neurons

Another bit of recent neuroscience research which has caused a stir recently could also add to our understanding of how relationship works on the neurological level. This is research into 'mirror neurones', originally conducted in Macaque monkeys.

This research demonstrated how neurons can fire in sympathy from one monkey to another, simply on the basis of watching an action. A monkey observes another monkey picking up a stick. The stick-picking-up neurons of the observing monkey fire, just as they do for the monkey who actually handles the stick. Daniel Glaser has demonstrated the same phenomenon in humans using MRI images of the brains of dancers watching videos of a dance form they are trained in and of one they are not trained in. As would be predicted by the Macaque experiments, the relevant neurons fired more during the familiar than the unfamiliar routine.

This demonstrates the capacity of the brain to mirror actions we see in others, and has been taken as a demonstration of empathy at work. This could be the neuronal level of the sort of communication between minds that has been noted throughout this book, starting with some simple crowd examples in Chapter 2. The argument of the book is that this sort of communication, as distinct from explicit, verbal or other signed, communication is the province of the relational subsystem.

Conclusion of the excursion into neuroscience.

So, why am I not more excited by these fascinating, up to date, findings of neuroscience? Why do I not see them as key to the God dilemma, if not at this very moment, at least in the near future? The answer is that though these neuroscience findings are at a level of minute detail and extremely accurate at that level, what they tell us about the wider picture is sort of obvious. It is nice to be able to understand the mechanism for things like the fear response, and empathy. However, we already know that the fear response and empathy exist. This research helps us to see how they are produced at the neuronal level. Similarly, the research into the brain correlates of mystical and prayerful experiences is interesting, but do not tell us anything we did not know. In the case of the debate between believers and sceptics, they seem to entrench people in their respective bunkers. It is at the level of meaning making; of construing as Kelly would put it, that we humans put our stamp on things. ICS is about meaning making.

I have to admit that ICS is a lot less exact than this neuroscience research. At the start of this chapter, I made it clear that the cognitive science research findings, on which it is based, though voluminous, can be interpreted in different ways. However, I would argue that the ICS hypothesis of the two, independent, organizing subsystems does give us a new way of making sense of a lot of puzzling data. Furthermore, it makes sense at the level of complexity and sophistication where meaning making kicks in. It is for these reasons that I base my argument on ICS rather than on neuroscience.

Objections to this Model

Let us return to the main line of argument that I derive from ICS, and in particular, to objections to it. I have been floating these ideas about how ICS can be used to understand what is going on in both spiritual experience and psychosis in talks and writings for long enough now to know that some people will be feeling distinctly uncomfortable about the line I am taking. Some will be downright angry. (Of course, the seriously angry will have given up long ago.) Am I really suggesting that there is absolutely no difference between the most sublime states of mysticism, accessed by the greatest saints and sages throughout the ages on the one hand – and the ravings of a lunatic or the trip of a junkie on the other? And that it all boils down to a matter of cognitive processing and states of arousal? Well, yes and no.

Of the contemporary examples I have chosen in order to explore the transliminal in detail, two are ecstatic and unitive, but with some problem elements. The third clearly describes madness, but there are areas of overlap with the other two. I am not the only person to have recognised this area of overlap as significant and worthy of study. Mike Jackson's research explores this topic thoroughly, for instance. As outlined earlier, for detailed analysis he has chosen individuals who sit firmly on that borderline between spiritual experience and madness. His writings are listed in the books to refer to at the end of this volume, and I recommend them to anyone interested in more data on this subject.

My emphasis has been on overlap, because until recently, most literature on this subject has started from a way of construing psychosis and spirituality that assumes they are distinct, and proceeds to explore the differences. This limitation of perspective has ensured that the concept of the transliminal has been incompletely grasped. My argument is that grasping this concept fully and in all its aspects, lies at the heart of making sense of the universality of the sacred and religion in human culture.

This does not mean that I ignore the importance of the factors that determine whether someone's transliminal experience will be joyful and enlightening; briefly disturbing but essentially manageable, or the prelude to the sort of psychotic breakdown that can permanently derail the individual's life. These factors and ways to manage them lie at the heart of my work as a therapist.

I have already said that the groundedness and maturity of the individual making the journey will have a lot to do with the outcome, and that such experiences have the potential to be life enhancing and transformative - importantly they can open the way to compassionate action and artistic creation. However, I have not shrunk from painting the flip side of personal disintegration, and failure to be able to operate in the shared world; in other words, madness.

So, I recognise very different possible outcomes to transliminal experiences. Which way it goes depends on a lot of factors, such as containing context as well as personal qualities. Chance could have a role here too. What I refuse to say, and what will upset some people, is that the area of experience separates into two intrinsically different parts.

There are theories held by some (but not all) transpersonal psychologists, and based on certain religious traditions, that the transliminal is rigidly divided into different layers or dimensions. These are hierarchically organised into higher and lower, and that the lower are accessed in madness, and the higher in spiritual and unitive experience. Ken Wilber is an influential contemporary exponent of this view.

According to this model, there are two incompatible ways of construing the situation of a person (like Annabel for instance) who undergoes a spiritual experience which takes a turn for the uncontrollable and paranoid so that they end up in a mental health hospital with a diagnosis. First construction: the diagnosis is wrong; it was a spiritual emergency, to use Stanislav Grof's term (which was discussed in relation to Catherine's account), not a psychosis! Sue the hospital! Second construction: it wasn't a real spiritual experience at all, just the illusion of one, because the person was mad and so accessing a much lower level of the transliminal. The trouble is that both constructions describe the same scenario. In the light of the examples I gave in Chapter 7, I would argue that such a distinction is likely to be completely arbitrary.

The problem with this way of construing for me is the same as my problem with life after death. How do they know? Some of the regularities of transliminal experience have been outlined in the previous chapter, but they are hardly reassuringly predictable. Things shift and change. One minute it is Mama, the next it is an owl. One minute it is bliss. The next it is terror. How do you make a neat map out of that? This is a place radically beyond our boundary making ability. The Propositional mind delights in maps, but is scared by the uncontrollability of the transliminal. I put hierarchical models of the spiritual world in the same box as diagnostic categories – ways of warding off the anxiety that the full force of the transliminal produces.

Also, the human tendency to assume that human beings occupy a place at the centre of the universe has always been a fertile source of error. – witness the prolonged resistance to the idea that the earth goes round the sun! To my mind, the ICS model convincingly reveals that we experience the world in two radically different ways, the ordinary and the transliminal, because of the way our brains are organised. The split is in us – not out there. It is more conventional to view these phenomena as experiencing other realities, other dimensions etc. that are outside ourselves. It can feel a bit of a come down to accept that we are simply getting two stabs at the same environment, and that both ways of accessing it are intrinsically incomplete.

Having got the religious/spiritual/transpersonal lobby thoroughly upset, I am soon going to annoy the scientists, by suggesting that both ways of knowing, the propositionally founded, logical one, and the mystical, mad, transliminal one, are important and valid. In order to make way for that argument I need to say a bit more about the relational subsystem and the self.

A major underlying theme of the next few chapters will be on the lines of; things are not necessarily what they seem; comfortable assumptions need to be examined, and the values that really matter are often sacrificed by following the obvious agenda. The Robb Johnson song slipped in here illustrates these themes for me; it highlights what we have lost in terms of way of life by pursuing economic goals which have compromised fundamental values. It captures that sense of fault-line and incompleteness that runs through the book. As usual, there is a complex mix of themes which I do not intend to unpack. A lot of highly transliminal symbolic references (Babylon, Jerusalem, holy grail – possibly a few too many!) It also harks forward to the Twyford Down section at the end of the next chapter. And, I thought things were getting a bit heavy, so that it was time to take a brief holiday with some verse ....do skip it if you think it is a bit long!

St. Ive's End Lane.

It was always Summer.
The sea and sky were blue.
The woods and lanes around St. Ive's End Lane,
Were cool and dark and green .

The lane was sand and potholes.
(My great aunt's best friend lived in an old railway carriage).
Everything was overgrown,
And cool and dark and green.

Now the motorway runs through Twyford Down.
Oh, there's a Tesco outside every town.
And everywhere looks much the same,
As nowhere fast at all.

By the roadside of Babylon
I wept.
Where has Jerusalem gone?

It took all day to get to.
The landscape of childhood.
Cream tea model villages,
Wild horses in the wood.

We went by bus to Bournemouth once.
It was just too far away.
We used to walk to Ringwood town
When it was market day.

Now we wonder where it went so wrong,
Whose fault?
It was there all along,
That sent us

Into exile
To sing a transport song.

By the roadside.....

We had the best intentions.
All you had to do
Was do your best,
And life would
More or less work out for you.

We thought the war was over.
We thought the wound would heal.
We had the Beatles and the Welfare State.
None of it was real.

Now I've seen that holy citadel,
No glory, hope,
No holy grail.
Just bloodstains
In a bullring
Where the heart of England fell.

By the roadside....

Yet, I still walk the big hill,
Fields move like the sea.
But St. Ive's End Lane is not the place
My childhood used to be.

Nice cars commute to London,
Neat white bungalows,
The new town nuclear children
They got nowhere left to go,

'Cause the motorway runs through Twyford Down.
Oh, there's a Tesco outside every town,
And everywhere looks much the same
As nowhere fast at all.

By the roadside ......

Robb Johnson 'The Night Café' CD.

CHAPTER 11

Shifting the Centre of Gravity – Towards Relationship

We have now tracked that 'other' way of experiencing, the transliminal, through the journeys into madness or extreme spiritual experience of our adventurers, and have used this to understand more about how the transliminal works. This concept of the transliminal has then been tied into what we know about the workings of the brain, both at the level of neurons, and, more tellingly, at the level of the higher organization of the pathways of the brain; in particular, those pathways concerned with meaning making.

To someone like myself, who has always been fascinated by the 'spiritual' dimension of experience, unpacking what lies behind it appears vital and important. I am aware that here I do not speak for everyone. It is my object in writing this book to interest people in general; not just the hymn singers and tree huggers (which includes me); not just the religious, the eccentric and actually or potentially mad!

So, what has the transliminal to do with the 'ordinary person'? Someone who is not particularly spiritual; who does not quite see the point of religion, and is definitely not mad and is determined that it should stay that way? Making this connection between spiritual/religious experience and madness; emphasizing the way in which they exist side by side, like the snakes and seraphs of the William James quotation, could be distinctly off-putting to such sensible, pragmatic individuals.

This book is not so much giving information about madness or belief, as arguing that taking a fresh look at madness and belief, and its shared psychological basis, sheds a whole new and radical light on the human being. At the core of this new perspective is the idea that the human being does not make sense in isolation. We only make sense in the context of a web of relationship. To see human beings in this light requires a huge shift in perception. The whole centre of gravity of the person needs to move from the individual towards the wider context in which the individual operates. More challenging, I am going to argue that this is a two way process. As well as the web making sense of us, the way in which we relate in this web shapes who we are.

So what constitutes this web? The 'friends and family' list on the phone are obviously core to anyone's web, plus those who would be on our list if they weren't dead. But the web spreads far further than that. As well as embracing our ancestors (whose role in the living community has been better appreciated by other cultures), it includes those who come after us; the transliminal does not recognize time. This web takes in all our wider 'belong-ingness' – to group, neighbourhood, profession, nation, the human race. It spreads wider than that – to our non human ancestors and co-inhabitants of the planet – the animals, birds, fishes and insects; it extends to the earth itself. I am now going to develop the argument that this web of relationship is both at the core of who we are, and is the key to understanding the persis-tence of spirituality, the survival of God.

The Rationality Assumption Revisited.

How do I get there? It is time to recall the two basic assumptions identified in Chapter 2, as they lie at the root of that unexamined, shared, construct of a human being which I am questioning. Let us re-examine these assumptions in the light of what we now know about the transliminal from our travellers, and about the human mind from ICS.

The first assumption says that rationality is pre-eminent and more important than experience. ICS really helps us to see clearly what is going on here, and why this is such a difficult argument to get to grips with.

At the heart of ICS is the 'crack' between the two central meaning making systems. The propositional, which can only operate in close co-operation with the relational, is in charge of verbally based rationality; either-or logic. It tends to assume superiority, because of its command of that self conscious sense of self which we again, assume, is 'I'; *the* 'self' – because that is what it feels like. ICS lets us into the secret – that there is no overall boss; that the command in fact passes backwards and forwards, and even when the propositional is in charge 'front of house', the relational could well be pulling the strings in the background.

The psychoanalysts from Freud onwards, who identified the extent of the influence of the unconscious on our decisions and our lives, had uncovered that one. This could be conceded, and it could still be argued that the rational, logical, propositional 'should' be in charge. The relational, with its wayward, irrational, influence, ought to be kept in check. That is certainly how Freud saw the 'Id', the subconscious part of the person.

In a situation where the person is viewed as a balancing act (as in ICS), such straightforward 'shoulds' and 'oughts' come into question. Put all your weight on one side of the balance and the thing will topple over! Yes, the relational if not checked by the propositional, can lead the individual into dark and dangerous places. There are plenty of examples of that in Matthew's account, for instance. However, we have also seen that all the things we value most, such as the relationships with those we love, depend on the relational subsystem, and on the relational way of knowing.

It is because of that separation, explained by ICS, between the two central subsystems that they cannot properly comprehend each other. They operate in different modalities. They are chalk and cheese. I think that this is what creates the frustration. It also produces that sense of mystery without which our world would be greatly the poorer.

We know so much – we have the sense that we should be able to grasp it all fully; to explain it; to pin it down. When the relational knowledge, which we encounter through experience and emotion, proves to be subtly out of reach of our logical minds, we are then inclined to downgrade it; to say it is inferior and less important. I think the truth is that both are important; vitally important, but we are unable to grasp both in the same way and within the same system. This is not because there is any sort of split in reality (as we tend to argue in our arrogance). The split is in ourselves as the measuring instrument. If we can take that on board; accept it (and it is hard for us to accept imperfection), this information can have profound implications for our ability to make sense of some of the most puzzling aspects of our world.

The Billiard Ball Mind Assumption again

The second assumption was the 'billiard ball mind' assumption. How does ICS help here? Recall that this one says that human beings are self contained within their physical boundaries. In particular, it identifies the mind with the brain and so locates the mind firmly within the skull. This is the point at which I take ICS further than its inventors or its other proponents, but I do believe it has the potential to open a new perspective on the role of relationship and connection at the heart of our selves. This perspective convinces me because it makes sense of so many aspects of life that are not well explained otherwise. In order to explore this, let us look at the place of the relational in our lives.

In ordinary life, moving between the dominance of either of the two subsystems is like breathing. We shift backwards and forwards all the time. Sometimes we are more focused. At such times, the propositional is well engaged. Then we drift and daydream and the relational takes over. At such times the transliminal, the threshold, is closer, but the real crossing of the threshold takes place when the propositional is truly left behind.

It has long been noted that leaps of creative thinking take place at times of disengaged attention – from the time of Archimedes on, baths, showers and toilets have been recognized as occasions for that crucial breakthrough. The way I see it, when the propositional is well engaged, we are somehow locked in our individual selves. Liberated from this, we are open to relationship with that which is beyond us. We are free to make contact with other minds; other influences. This means letting in those influences, which carries risks as well as bonuses.

This is how we grow and develop as people, by absorbing from the new and the other. I see the attraction of travelling to exotic places as a way of expanding ourselves by providing novel stimuli to assimilate. An interesting book or a new relationship can have a similar effect. Where the impact is great, the door to the transliminal is opened. Real growth is possible, but we become vulnerable to real pain and danger. If we open too far, we might fall apart. Falling in love is a universal example of this type of opening.

It goes deeper. As a therapist, I am only too aware of the way in which people are shaped by their important, early, relationships with parents and those around them. Almost inevitably these involve distortion, and distortion involves pain. Is there such a thing as perfectly balanced parenting? I doubt it! I certainly didn't manage it! Those distortions are carried around inside the person as a part of themselves. They tend to be self perpetuating as they are 'transferred' from one relationship to another – an example I referred to earlier.

This much is well recognized in a number of schools of therapy. Kleinians speak of 'internalized objects' – meaning the other person in the relationship, and Cognitive Analytic Therapy (one of my modalities) calls this 'Reciprocal Roles' – two way patterns of relating that are so much part of the individual's make-up that they keep cropping up. For instance, someone with an internalized 'controlling – controlled' reciprocal role has the uncanny knack of getting the most laid back of individuals to behave in a controlling way towards them. Therapy is a chance to re-examine and revise such patterns so that the person has a chance to develop new and healthier ways of relating, and so grow and flourish.

We have seen in discussing the transliminal, how boundaries dissolve when this state is entered, and the more someone is centred in their relational potential, the more they lose grip on their individuality and become part of the whole. I think this gives us a clue as to what is going on here. The billiard ball mind assumption offers us a construct of relationship which involves separate entities colliding – and then maybe cosying up to one another (even billiard balls can be in contact!) I think we badly need a different image (because we do think in pictures) but it is really hard to visualise this one. Jung's image of his dream of the collective unconscious in his autobiography, 'Memories, Dreams and Reflections' is quite telling. He dreamt of himself as a house, and descended to a cellar containing ancestral bones. If the individual cellars all connected underground that would help. However, that is all down and dark and transliminal connections can also be light and inspiring.

The person as both individual and part of the web.
The picture of the human being as dissolving into a web of relationship through their relational potential is literally impossible to visualise and therefore very hard to grasp. How can we be both individual and dissolve into other people; other beings; other things? It is impossible. It does not add up. That is the point. The information we get from our two different subsystems simply does not add up. It is like trying to add numbers and mud! The myths quoted earlier led us to this same place. The myths of the

garden of Eden, and of Prometheus, said that as human beings we are in-between gods and animals, and this feels unsatisfactory, incomplete and at times, downright painful.

The paradox is, that the transliminal, the place where we are closest to the gods, is also where we are closest to the animals and to the baby – both of whom have poorly developed propositional subsystems (or none, depending on how far down the evolutionary hierarchy you go). How do we make sense of that and fit it into a tidy system? The answer is that we don't. Maybe all we can do is experience it.

In my case, it is experience that has convinced me of this perspective. Coming across ICS has simply given me a framework for making sense of important experiences that I have noted throughout my life. One example was being on the periphery of those close to a fellow student who died in a road traffic accident at the age of nineteen. At the same time as fighting with the horror of this event; that life, so full of potential, snuffed out in an instant, I was aware of those close to her; her sister, her parents and her boyfriend, welded together in the love they felt for her. That love was tangible to me from the outside. At the same time, I knew (but not rationally) that her love for them was also at the heart of it – no less real and vital for her no longer inhabiting her body on this earth.

What I now know of the transliminal and its ability to transcend time and physicality enables me to make a little more sense of this powerful experience. My understanding of the relational mind suggests to me that she was still a vital part of those close to her, through that aspect of their joint selves, and they of her. Just don't ask me precisely how!

So, love and death can open that crack and let us see and experience the operation of the transliminal in our lives. This can be a powerful force for growth and transformation. It can also be painful and even potentially dangerous. I would like now to offer another, more recent, instance from my own life of this sort of growth, expansion and pain through my experience of opening myself to the other. For me this came about through falling in love; falling in love with a landscape, and one that was doomed to be destroyed.

Twyford Down

I live in Southampton, and the ancient cathedral city of Winchester lies about eight miles to the North – capital of England in King Alfred's day as legend has it. Between these two cities run the great sweep of undulating chalk downland that graces the South of Britain. St. Catherine's hill in Winchester is justly famous as a sacred site, crowned by its graceful grove of trees. Next to it lies deep Plague Pit Valley, where the bodies of the plague victims of Winchester were flung in those dark times. Next to that there was once Twyford Down. Now there is a huge, hideous and obscene scar in the chalk, through which cars and lorries constantly thunder, projecting their noise and fumes, as the road has a particularly steep incline, throughout the city of Winchester.

It was a long time coming, this abomination. It is a devious tale, full of betrayal and corruption, and the careful preservation of a bottleneck in the road between Southampton and London at Winchester to help force through this unacceptable solution. Well attended rallies were held against the proposal, backed by the great and the good and the environmental lobby groups. It was going to be alright. Then an unexpected electoral outcome meant that the party wanting the road were returned to power. The unthinkable became inevitable. The opposition accepted reality and melted. Except…

A small band of direct action protesters had set up camp on the proposed site of the road to prevent construction. This remarkable group called themselves the Dongas Tribe after the deep gullies between the downs, made by the passage of people and flocks through the ages at the great crossing point of routes that was Winchester. They, along with many committed allies from the respectable citizens of Winchester and Southampton, opened my heart, my capacity to relate, so that this landscape became as precious; more precious even, than human life. For me, this has been an infinitely enriching experience. In embracing the earth in this very particular way I am expanded and at the same time merged. For me, my family, and our Creation Spirituality/ GreenSpirit group, joining with the Dongas to protest at the outrage has also been a life changing experience.

The camp on Twyford Down was a welcoming place in the autumn of 1992. The benders and tipis that were home to the group blended into the land. The kettle boiled on the fire. The campers sang chants, made banners and mended the pantomime dragon that was such an effective part of their regular disruption of the construction (destruction) work – difficult to arrest, a pantomime dragon! Music, theatre and humour were part of the spirit and the method of the protest. Our group contributed by leading dances with live music at one of the big rallies, and composing the 'Twyford Litany'.

But this was not a jolly outing. The Dongas were woken at dawn and brutally thrown off the land by the 'yellow men' (from their visibility clothing) of the security company. Once the road building was underway in earnest, there was razor wire, there were arc lights, and I once witnessed two hundred policemen marching down a hillside to eject protesters sitting on a temporary bridge, to prevent it being put across the road, as part of the construction plan. Protesters with resources were targeted with punitive injunctions, through information gleaned by a (gloriously dim-witted) private detective agency.

Personally, my heart was opened to previously unplumbed depths of pain, sorrow and rage. I always knew that if anything happened to either of my sons or my husband, I would be devastated. I had not realised I could feel the same way about the rape of a landscape. My commitment to an environmentally sensitive lifestyle, at least in terms of transport, has measurably deepened.

My new job of three years is eight miles from home. I cycle there, using the bus (with my folding bike) for part of the way back. This might not save the planet, but apart from being a life and health enhancing choice for me, it is visible, so does make people think.

The protest failed to stop the road. The road building programme itself continued, but the tide of public revulsion that essentially started with Twyford did eventually bring it to a halt. Where the reasoned argument of the major environmental movements and the political process had failed, the power of the relational/ the transliminal had been harnessed. Hearts had been opened and lives changed. This was in the true sense a spiritual experience.

To conclude this with the second part of a poem by Andrew Jordan, the poet who has captured the movement in his powerful book of poems: 'The Mute Bride.' Many of these poems echo the themes I have identified of a cosmic desecration – it was hard to choose which one to include.

M3

The scar in the hillside
is permanent now. Surreal
it casts the quality of dream
a trauma of memories,

over the valley. The chalk
white face of a child
newly abused. Vaginal
entrance to the underworld

where Orpheus commits
his accidental act
of betrayal (over and over)
His fate acting out in him

inadvertently. Damsel flies
the black gloss of their wings,
swarm. Even in a dream
it seems impossible to turn

these symbols into anything
really powerful. Regrets,
the dark feminine water,
cannot be reconciled.

Andrew Jordan. 'The Mute Bride'. P. 78-79.

To knit this digression into the general argument: I am claiming that the experience of Twyford Down represented an opening to the transliminal; to mystery. The sense of abomination and revulsion around what was done there felt like sacrilege and the desecration of something holy. This sense of desecration was shared by all involved, including people from a variety of religions and no religion. I am further claiming that, on a personal level, the experience was transformative – not just in terms of life choices but in terms of an expansion and opening of the self. The folding bike is merely a visible result of this inner event. How do I know? I feel it. Not very scientific! Now I will try and link this feeling with what I have learnt about the self from ICS.

The web and the self

The self is something we normally take for granted. When we think about it, the inner and outer ways of knowing apply to the self as much as to religion. We collect evidence of how we stand in the world, and are viewed by others, whether in the form of the annual appraisal at work, or from the sort of looks they give us. This evidence affects how we feel about ourselves. We are piecing together our construct of 'our self'. It can appear to be a firm rock, there for all time, or it can collapse like a flimsy scaffolding when hit by the blast of a major trauma or crushing shame. We started to build this picture of ourselves as viewed from the outside from the age of two or before; from the time when we first realised that some of the things we did were not acceptable to others....

This sense of self from the outside is produced by the propositional and relational subsystems working together to build up a picture. However, our relational subsystem, which is the more fundamental of the two, and the one that connects our senses with our body's arousal system, is continually looking out for the status of the self. This is not cool, theoretical knowledge; it is hot and vital. Are we secure in our important relationships? Are we safe? Are we accepted? Are we surrounded by friends and family or by foes? Are we going to eat or be eaten? We register the answers to these questions in our gut reaction. While everything is the same as usual, this vigilance doesn't bother us, but put us into an unfamiliar, potentially hostile situation and it is a different story.

This automatic emotional reaction, organized by the relational subsystem, is essentially about our relationship with ourselves. Relationship makes up the very stuff of our selves; we could almost say we *are* a relationship. The same emotional response that we know about through the physical arousal reaction, organizes our relationships with those outside of ourselves. Emotions are catching. They operate beyond the individual – whether the excitement of the football match, the anger of the lynch mob, or simply the frosty atmosphere in the family when something has gone badly wrong.

We have already noted that the transliminal operates beyond the individual. The transliminal experiences recounted earlier abound with examples of the self merging with something greater, and a sense of invasion of the self from the outside. As discussed earlier in this chapter, when the relational subsystem has got free of the propositional, the boundaries of the individual start to dissolve. For most of us, this is very relative, as in the sense of being one with a group or a crowd. A little alcohol can help this dissolution along in a pleasant fashion. For our travellers into the transliminal of the earlier chapters, the experience of going beyond the self was more extreme.

Another way of viewing this is through the perspective of the growing child. For a baby, its parents are all important. It cannot exist without their support, and the baby only gradually works out where caregiver ends and it begins. The attitude of those around it has a profound effect on the baby's development. John Bowlby and the whole body of literature and research on what is called 'Attachment' have proved that conclusively. There is a sense in which those important relationships are a part of that individual baby. This can stay with the person throughout their life. As noted when ideas about internalized relationships were covered, the function of therapy is to provide a corrective experience where harmful or unhelpful relationships have become part of the person in early life.

This is where the argument about the self, and the way in which the self develops through relationship with self and others, meets the idea of the web of relationship. The people around the baby are also part of other people. Through their relational subsystems, they are profoundly influenced by their culture and social group. The quality of that relationship will make a profound difference to their being. Despised minorities take the attitudes of others deeply into themselves, which is why discrimination and racism are such damaging forces.

Other relationships affect and shape us, as we in our turn shape them. Our relationship with the non-human animals has always been a crucial and deeply ambiguous one. On the one side we idolise them as pets; our ancestors worshipped them as gods, and they appear as powerful archetypal figures in our dreams. On the other side, our treatment of them is often appalling and diminishes us, whether through factory farming, or through allowing a degradation of the environment that wipes out whole species year by year.

If our relationship with the animals is cause for shame, our relationship with the earth is that and more. We rob and despoil the soil, the air, the water, the minerals; every part of our beautiful and sustaining planet. We know we are ruining the planet. We know we are robbing our children and their children. My argument is that we are twisting and distorting our very selves by our reckless greed. Because we fail to understand this vital connection, we do not see it like that. It is a problem that is 'out there'. Our consciences might or might not prod us to do something about it. The aim of the extended section on my own relationship with Twyford Down was intended to illustrate the impact on myself of a growing awareness of that vital and integral relationship to the earth and landscape. Because of that experience it is no longer one I can ignore.

I have here attempted to consolidate the idea that the individual person is only partially an individual person. The propositional holds that sense of individuality, but in our relational selves, we are in a very real sense a part of the whole. When we access the transliminal in the sort of minor ways we all do – sunsets and the like – we glimpse that. Those who fully cross the threshold for real, experience themselves as lost in the whole – or as being the whole. All this is beyond what our propositional, logical minds can fully grasp – but relationship is something you feel; not something you know through logic. We can feel more than we can precisely know. That is what I meant when I stated earlier that I felt that allowing myself to be open to relationship to Twyford Down had expanded and deepened my self, not least in my capacity to hold and experience pain.

CHAPTER 12

Ideas and Power: Spotting the Transliminal at Work

The previous chapter tracked the way in which we as human beings are more complex, more entwined and more responsible than we perhaps thought we were, because of the way in which we are partly relationship. Like the frogs in my pond, we are amphibians. We can either hop on the solid ground of ordinary logic and well understood reality, or swim in the enticing, ever shifting waters of the transliminal. We find ourselves in the transliminal way of experiencing when we leave well behind that firm (but limiting) foothold that our propositional subsystem allows us. But we are forever dipping in and out of the waters (more like the birds that bathe in the pond, actually) as we go about our everyday lives.

In the last chapter I suggested that until we take this aspect of our functioning seriously we will not understand the individual person very well. In this chapter I am going to argue that we need to become better at spotting the transliminal at work in order to make sense of a variety of vital aspects of our world. Even if the transliminal only glances in and out of our lives, it plays an important part, whether we see ourselves as spiritual or absolutely not.

This book gives central place to the accounts of the travellers just because this provided the basis for the breakdown of the characteristics of the transliminal. Being clear about these characteristics helps us to spot the transliminal at work. Whether we realize it or not, it is probably influencing our values and life choices in profound ways. The more we understand the nature of this influence, the more we can reflect upon it, using the capacity for intelligent thought afforded by our propositional subsystem. This should not lead us to automatically cancel the transliminal/relational influence, but rather to enable us to make clear sighted choices.

These insights are not new. The psychoanalysts make the same point using the un/subconscious terminology. The term transliminal merely enables me to widen the scope of the argument, and get away from the judgements implied by the earlier terms.

Recognizing the transliminal at work.

So, we need to be able to spot the transliminal at work. What do we look for? I will now build on the list of characteristics of the transliminal that arose out of the accounts of those journeying in this region. I will use these characteristics to identify signs of the transliminal at work in the everyday world. This will lead to examination of three important areas, namely politics, creativity and mystery, in a bit more detail with some examples.

The main topics we dealt with in chapter eight were: loss of boundaries; sense of mission; transliminal (both-and) logic; the numinous; conviction; cosmic suffering and supernatural entities.

- *Loss of boundaries* can be spotted in loss of a sense of proportion. A common example of this is the scale of remuner-ation commanded by pop and sports stars. It is commonly argued that such packages are determined by the market. This is supposed to be a rational, scientific, way of regulating reward. However, it is fairly clear that there is nothing partic-ularly rational about such disproportionate reward.

- Taking *sense of mission* and unshakable *conviction* together, these come from the supernatural and 'numinous' character of the experience. Out of context, these features can be unnerving; we tend to be wary of people with unshakable conviction and a sense of mission, and even doubt their sanity! However, where people with such a sense of mission manage to slot themselves seamlessly into the roles in our society that sanction such attributes, they are more likely to be reinforced than avoided. Suitable roles would be those of: great leader (political or spiritual); famous artist; star (music, sport, screen etc.) The fact that so many people may be willing to hand over control and even their identity to such figures says something about the way the construct of the self can just dissolve – see loss of boundaries, the previous point!

• The sensitivity to *cosmic suffering* noted in the accounts of the adventurers translates into the sort of altruistic empathy that represents the best in people; the outpouring of generosity at a time of disaster; the sort of selfless vocation that motivates people to volunteer to serve in places like disaster areas; to work sacrificially for their fellow beings in circumstances where most people would turn away. But the impulse to turn away can also be linked to this aspect. Because this type of empathy feels so open, so raw and so vulnerable, it can be unbearable, and can cause the opposite reaction of shutting down and hardening the heart.

• *The numinous.* Otto's description of 'mysterium tremendum' might not immediately strike a chord in terms of everyday occurrences. However, the attraction of strange and inexplicable occurrences is common enough. As with the sensitivity of the last example, there are two sides to this. It can represent a rather shallow seeking after a 'wow' experience. At its worst, it leads people to ignore common sense explanations in order to hang onto the wow. This sort of thing gives the supernatural a bad name! On the other hand, it also points to that sense of the sacred that encounter with mystery that produces awe and reverence in the beholder. This, I would argue, is something real and valuable, which will be explored further.

• Encountering *supernatural entities* is not an everyday occurrence – though plenty of people have had some sort of a ghost experience, or recount meeting with a loved one who has recently died.

• All these features exhibit the paradoxical, *both-and logic* that is characteristic of the transliminal. This aspect is inescapably part of human thought, because our relational subsystem is an inescapable part of us. Yet it is an aspect that has attracted some interesting adverse publicity. I will next turn attention to this, as an example of the problems of not understanding the centrality of this feature of human information processing.

Associative thinking and memes.

To start with the both-and logic; we have seen that this works on the principle of connection or association rather than analysis. As mentioned earlier, Matte Blanco calls this 'symmetric logic'. Because of this faculty of association, which is deeply embedded in our thinking, the very words we use to identify something with precision can carry with them a host of other echoes that we possibly did not intend, and which can confuse the message. I have already noted this tendency for words to carry baggage with them - for instance, 'subconscious' conjures up subways, substandard etc. and so is not helpful for me in talking about spirituality.

As Matte Blanco was a psychoanalyst he did not have a problem with this logic as he recognized it as a property of the unconscious, and psychoanalysts are quite comfortable with the sub/unconscious! However, other commentators have identified this associative feature of human thought as a source of trouble. For instance, Steve Hayes, has developed a very practical form of therapy called 'Acceptance and Commitment Therapy' based on a radical distrust of language. He distrusts language because of the way words carry with them all sorts of uncontrollable, emotionally volatile, associations – a bit like taking in an infectious germ when drinking apparently pure, but in fact contaminated, water.

Richard Dawkins sees the associative power of language in this way too. As an evolutionary biologist, Dawkins is an expert on genes, and fascinated by their power to replicate. In his book 'The Selfish Gene' he suggested that the way in which ideas took hold, replicated and had a life of their own was just like genes - so he called them 'memes'. However, because the 'successful' (in Darwinian terms) ideas are often ones that Dawkins deplores, such as religion and ideology, he has argued that these particular memes behave like viruses. This vivid image introduces a whole raft of rather sinister and frightening associations – thanks to the associative ability of our relational mind!

Richard Dawkins is the inspiration for a little group of academics and commentators with a mission to defend the two assumptions that this book seeks to undermine; the rationality assumption and the billiard ball mind assumption. Prominent among them are Sue Blackmore and Daniel Dennet. I am sure there are others, but I am aware that these three have adopted the 'meme' concept with enthusiasm, as a way of turning ideas into 'things' and getting rid of the intractable, mysterious, bit from the idea of consciousness. My argument is simply that the waywardness of associative thinking, and the mysterious nature of consciousness are written into our hardware, and even the brightest minds of the generation will be unable to argue them away.

The way that human thinking is made up of two incompatible logics does indeed introduce a host of problems. Muddle and confusion do tend to reign where the two incompatible logics bump into each other. This means that it is very hard to pin down this whole area scientifically. Hard facts prove elusive and dogma and unfounded assertion tend to take over, whether in defending or attacking the spiritual and supernatural. The transliminal has an unfortunate way of combining absolute certainty with a hazy grasp of reality on the ground.

The gift of power

Understanding the transliminal can also help us to get a handle on the way human beings seem to give away their power to others. This phenomenon illustrates both the *dissolution of boundaries* and the *sense of mission* characteristics identified at the beginning of the chapter. The whole of history is full of megalomaniac rulers and abject subjects. Hitler became chancellor of Germany through a democratic election (and a bit of wheeling and dealing). He was then in a position to change the constitution to give himself more power – a familiar story. Nazism is an excellent example of the clever use of the transliminal; an ideology of national renewal, hammered home through the inspiring rituals of the Nuremburg rallies. Swept along by the transliminal tide, people's rational faculty was blunted to the appalling crimes being perpetrated in their name. Even today, Germany is coming to terms with how it could have handed over its power to this monster, back in the last century.

To what extent is this an inescapable part of human nature, and to what extent do we have to take some responsibility for handing over our individual power to these tyrants? This is a difficult question, as with all transliminally driven processes, things can change very quickly to their opposite, and the subjects can turn against their rulers. Events such as the collapse of East Germany and the fall of the Ceaucescus in Romania demonstrate that rulers are often unable to stand against a determined and united opposition. On the other hand, resisting a tyrannical regime can lead to a heavy cost in human life and freedom. The crushing of another protest movement by the brutal regime in Burma in September/October 2007 demonstrates this cost, born heavily by the monks of that country and their supporters.

Nazism is an extreme, but by no means an isolated example of the way in which the transliminal operates in politics. Whenever ideology is on the agenda, we do well to examine it, before deciding whether to be swept up or not. Going back over the 'modern' (i.e. post medieval) period of history, behind the careful construction of nationalism lay the agenda of getting people to hand their power over, willingly, to the absolute monarch. The doctrine of 'The Divine Right of Kings' that gained currency at that time (with a little help from the said monarchs) is an example of political hijacking of the transliminal.

Of course, the Romans and Egyptians with their deified rulers had hit on the same idea to consolidate their power. However, such is the seduction of the transliminal that they might well have believed in their own divinity. When the idea of absolute monarchy was being established in Europe, the apparatus of state, though brutal, was far less efficient and far reaching than today. Where religious splits started after the reformation, such rulers usually saw religious uniformity as essential. To allow religious diversity to flourish would let in rival ideologies, and undermine stability. Elizabeth I of England was unusual in applying the idea of a national church with a degree of flexibility, while working hard at the nationalist agenda.

This is too vast a subject to explore here, and we do well not to be complacent in our own age. After all, how is it that the rulers of the UK and the USA have managed to take their countries into a war in Iraq that the vast majority of both populations now reject? I suspect that transliminal associative logic makes much more sense of the arguments behind that particular venture than rational logic. Such arguments can, of course, be successfully deployed to mask straightforwardly economic considerations, like securing oil supplies.....

This is not to suggest that people always choose murderous dictators and dubious causes to give up their power to. People can choose to lose themselves in a noble cause, to dedicate their lives to a high ideal or to follow a saintly guru. The very extremes give us a clue that we are dealing with the transliminal, which fails to register the nuances of the confusingly ordinary. The transliminal deals in the highest and noblest, or the most despicable. We need our propositionally tempered wits about us to tell the difference, and to add in the shades of grey. The transliminal can lull us into a dangerous sleep of moral blindness.

Why do we give up our power?

Understanding the way in which the transliminal operates can be really helpful for unpacking why and how it is that human beings are so prone to hand over their power in this way. To get to the bottom of this, we need to return to the divided nature of the self as outlined in the previous chapters. The construct of the self might be pretty sure of itself, but underneath it needs the relational subsystem's work of constantly shoring it up. This system, connected as it is with the body's arousal system and the emotions, constantly scans the horizon for trouble. The horizon in this case is the individual's moment by moment position in the primate hierarchy of other human beings (present or absent – worrying about whether you said the wrong thing earlier, or how you will be received at a future encounter is just as concerning as walking into an actual tense situation).

In this world of status uncertainty, hanging onto the coat tails of the alpha male is obviously the safest strategy. But who is the alpha male in our unmanageably huge social structures? Who knows? With thousands and millions of people in this state of internal instability and volatility (while looking pretty sorted out on the surface), it is no surprise that news that the ultimate alpha male (or female) has been identified is catching. This is the source of that epidemic of abdication of personal power to anyone who manages to project the right image to capture the critical mass. In this situation success breeds success. It seems safer to back the winner.

This is an example of how relational minds can operate together. Rational calculation does not come into this process. Such calculation is usually brought in afterwards to find plausible arguments for a decision that has already been sewn up by the relational. After all, few things can be so undermining of a secure sense of self than the suspicion that you have just made a horrible error of judgement. Propositional and relational will work smoothly together to assure you that you were absolutely right in your choice. This phenomenon is borne out by a body of social psychological experimental data that reveals the human propensity to justify our choices after the event

Power and Magic

We have just reviewed the way in which the power of the transliminal insinuates itself into our ordinary psychology, and undermines the mastery of that independent individuality of which we are so proud. There are long held traditions that claim the art of harnessing this power of the transliminal in order to manipulate the physical world as well. Such arts tended to be passed on between members of sects sworn to secrecy, hence the general term 'occult' applied to such knowledge. Such power could be applied to healing, which puts it in line with widely accepted idea of faith healing. It was also sometimes employed in more dubious ways, as 'black arts'.

The Hermetic tradition of Hermes Trismegistus is one of the more respectable examples from late Greek culture, but this phenomenon had a tendency to surface all over the place, including in heretical Christian groups. Witchcraft, which survived in our culture as an underground form of the older religion, and today takes its place in the new age pantheon, is another example. Contemporary practitioners tend to stress the healing and benevolent use of this magic. Shamanic traditions similarly practice both magic and healing from power derived in ways understood only to the initiates. Shamanic rituals are interesting in both using psycho-active substances to attain the transliminal states necessary for such practices, and for their association with 'breakdown/breakthrough'. Suitability for shamanic apprenticeship was traditionally signalled by spontaneously accessing altered states of consciousness – which as we have seen can be a hazardous business.

Having opened up another huge area of discourse, I intend to close it down again and move on. This chapter has been about recognition of the operation of the transliminal in our world. We have seen how its various attributes can be spotted in aspects of human behaviour that we tend to take for granted. It is my contention that if we got better at noticing the transliminal at work, and tempering its influence with our propositional, the world would be a safer and a saner place. In the next two chapters, I will argue that without the influence of the transliminal on our culture, we would be unimaginably the poorer.

CHAPTER 13

Creativity and the Transliminal

The Night Cafe
A man could go mad here,
Commit any crime,
But mostly just sad men kill
Absinthe and time.
On the edge of some razor
Between sinner and saint,
On the edge of some masterpiece
They'll never paint:
In the night café.

. . . .

Crows in the wheatfield,
Boy in a jail.
Crows in the wheatfield,
All else fails.
But I thought you knew better:
What did God do?
To make you leave here,
And us without you,
In the night café .

Robb Johnson. From the CD 'The Night Café'

Creativity and Schizotypy

Creativity is a major pillar of the smug sense of superiority we carry around. It is big news when an animal or bird manages to use a stick to do something or other, and yet, look what we humans have achieved... Originality of thought and creative leaps of the imagination have characterised the great advances in science. Analytic, either-or, thinking might be essential for verification and consolidation but the great advances come when a gap opens up between the two main subsystems and insights from beyond are let in. A nice example of this is the way in which the chemist, Friedrich August Kekule, managed to specify the structure of the compound Benzine as made up from a ring of carbon atoms. The exact form of this compound had been eluding scientists for some time. It was only years later, when giving an after dinner speech that he let on how he had lighted on his discovery, as follows:

> "I was sitting writing on my textbook, but the work did not progress; my thoughts were elsewhere. I turned my chair to the fire and dozed. Again the atoms were gamboling before my eyes...My mental eye, rendered more acute by the repeated visions of the kind, could now distinguish larger structures of manifold conformation; long rows sometimes more closely fitted together all twining and twisting in snake-like motion. But look! What was that? One of the snakes had seized hold of its own tail, and the form whirled mockingly before my eyes. As if by a flash of lightning I awoke..."from Roberts, Royston M. *Serendipity, Accidental Discoveries in Science.*

In other words, he had dropped off at his work and dreamed the answer! Straight from the transliminal!

Artistic Creativity and Madness.

If this capacity to plumb the unconscious, the transliminal, is essential for the advancement of science, it is even more central to artistic creativity. There is also the recognized connection between creativity and madness, well illustrated by the artist, Van Gogh, who is featured in the Robb Johnson song at the beginning of this chapter, 'The Night Café' ('The Night Café', 'Crows in the Wheatfield' and 'Boy in a Jail' are all titles of famous paintings by Van Gogh). Van Gogh is famous for his highly original artistic vision, remarkable even in the late 19th century when artistic vision was being turned upside down on all sides by the impressionists and other modernists who followed them.

Van Gogh is also famous for operating on the borderline between sanity and madness. He succumbed to madness and an early death by suicide, but not before he had produced some of the most iconic paintings of the modern movement. More famous perhaps than those listed in the song are his 'Sunflowers'. It is probably no exaggeration to say that Van Gogh has forever shaped the way we see sunflowers: he has got under the skin of the construct of sunflowers for our age, with his intense rendering that particular bloom.

Creativity and madness do not inevitably go together. There are plenty of examples of great artists, writers etc. who were perfectly sane! This suggests to me that they were able to step beyond that threshold of ordinary experience, access the transliminal and utilize it in their art, and then return to ordinary life without losing their balance. Indeed, great art does need that connection with the propositional as well as the ability to move beyond it, if it is to have any success at communicating. The absinthe and late nights referred to in the song can just as easily destroy creativity as prime it. The artist who is too far lost in the transliminal, whether through substance use or naturally high schizotypy, will not get across to people in general (unless, as in the case of certain sorts of techno music, for instance, they are all on the same substance...)

In fact, creative expression can be the very factor that enables someone to navigate the more dangerous reaches of the transliminal, so that what might have resulted in madness becomes a transformative experience. I make the point about the connection between high schizotypy, creativity and vulnerability to psychosis when I run groups in the hospital where I work designed to help people cope with the symptoms of psychosis. I call the group the 'What is Real and What is Not' group.

The purpose of the group is threefold. Firstly, it is to help people to recognize that there are two distinct ways of experiencing. There are distinct advantages to knowing which you are in at any one time. This can be the basis for developing the ability to move from one to another at will. The second aim is to introduce and discuss methods of managing the threshold between the two ways of experiencing: methods such as arousal management and mindfulness. The third aim is to establish the idea that these sorts of experience are normal and associate them with valued areas such as creativity. As the stigma associated with a diagnosis like schizophrenia can be considerably more disabling than the condition itself, this boost to morale is possibly the most important part of the programme. As in all groups, there is the added bonus of people being able to share experiences, note their similarity, and so recognize that they are not alone.

The Artist beyond the Self; personae, inspiration and muses.

One example that I give in the group of the positive use of high schizotypy to avoid the dangers of madness is that of the pop singer David Bowie. David Bowie had a half brother who developed schizophrenia and eventually committed suicide. Bowie had been close to his older brother who was something of a role model. There are strong indications that Bowie's life might have followed a similar course, had he not exploited the way in which he sat lightly to his sense of self in order to take on the roles of various fantastical characters. A feature of his act was that he 'became' personae, such as Ziggy Stardust. A theme of coming from outer space ran through this phase of his career. His achievement was to do this in the context of a successful show business career rather than as a deluded mental patient. In this way, a highly communicative artistic creativity probably saved his sanity.

The Bowie example illustrates one way in which the loosening of the construct of the self in the transliminal can further artistic creation. If we look at the way in which artists and writers over the ages have described the process of creation, we can see that this is part of a wider phenomenon. The concept of 'inspiration' literally means 'breathing in', and is often used in a way that shades into the idea of possession. Possession has already been discussed in the context of that openness to outside influence that becomes possible when the relational subsystem is in control. Normally, the relational subsystem is held in check by the propositional with its sense of containment in individuality. When the relational takes charge, this containment is weakened, and the person can be open to influences beyond the individual.

Western literary culture has kept alive the idea of Muses who inspire artists. To the Greeks, these were minor goddesses in the retinue of Apollo, who brought inspiration to the artist. In later times, it was more ambiguous whether the muse was a real person, possibly a sexual partner, or a supernatural being. However, the concept of creativity coming from outside the individual remained. As usual in the transliminal, there is an undifferentiated continuum between the individual feeling inspired, a creative state of near possession where the artist cannot necessarily recognize the source of his/her product, and channelling, where the writer is a mere vessel through whom the communication flows. Popular contemporary works such as 'Conversations with God' are examples of channelled writing.

The Lure and the Value of the Transliminal

The artist is therefore one of the supreme tightrope walkers between the propositional and relational subsystems. The successful artist harnesses that power of the transliminal and calls to the relational in the rest of us, shaking us out of well worn ways of seeing and experiencing the world. Cracking open our constructs, he or she transports us willingly into transliminal spaces, whether through sublime or rhythmic music, through unexpected visual or poetic perspectives, or by opening us to parallel lives through the imagination in fiction.

It is our potential to be transported beyond our individual selves and beyond our constructs that makes this possible. It is the attraction of the relational way of being and the lure of the transliminal that gives such a high value to artistic creativity. Of course, each one of us can tap into this potential for creativity; each one of us can delight our fellows with story or song, or adorn our homes or ourselves with artefacts of our own making. However, in our highly centralized, capitalist, culture, this faculty is largely handed over to the professionals. This is another example of our willingness to hand over our power, creative power this time, to others who are sanctioned 'alpha' individuals, as discussed in the last chapter. In economic terms, this results in fantastical sums of money changing hands over the ownership of the penniless Van Gogh's 'Sunflowers'.

The uneasy relationship between the transliminal and the ordinary world of commerce is well illustrated by the way in which art and creativity, essential elements in the life of society, are alternately heaped with absurd reward (as in pop star remuneration) or kept on near extinction funding (as with regional theatre). Whenever the '3 Rs', back to basics, school of education succeeds in pushing art and creativity aside in the school curriculum, a counter movement eventually gets it reinstated.

In this respect, art is in a similar position to religion and spirituality, though often cited by those who attack religion and spirituality as the acceptable face of the transliminal (to hijack a phrase). Art does not feed the population or advance technology. However, it can make money and definitely boosts tourism, so is attractive to hard headed business types. Our capitalist society distorts this universal attraction of the aesthetic and artistic impulse; this capacity to move beyond our 'selves' and draw on the wealth of the transliminal in creativity. It makes it into a commodity. The monetary values assigned to 'great art' are absurd, whereas unknown creative artists struggle unrewarded. Van Gogh's sunflowers sell for the sum equivalent to the gross national product of a small country, whereas, his brother Theo, who managed his business affairs, would have been lucky to sell them for enough to pay the rent in his lifetime.

Van Gogh did not have the chance to experience the effects of the fame and adulation he was to receive after his death. As with the political figures discussed in the previous chapter, the effect of receiving this exaggerated valuation can be dangerously distorting to the fragile balance of the individual self. Sensing oneself to be at the bottom of the primate hierarchy leads to anxiety and depression. Being at the top, and receiving the adulation of millions, can be even more destabilising and disturbing. Pop stars perhaps resort to hard drugs and destructive drinking in order to maintain that artificial high produced by mass adulation, as the crash from that plateau feels unbearable. Sports stars who take performance enhancing substances, despite the danger of humiliating consequences when found out, are maybe driven by fear of not maintaining those inflated expectations. Political leaders can start out as models of reasonableness, only to become isolated in an unreal world of power.

In an effect that is more widely damaging, the inflation of the star creator or performer can suck the innate creative impulse from the rest of us. Children happily paint and sing until they are taught that their productions, compared to these stars, are just not up to scratch, and they learn to be passive consumers for life – so adding to the inflation of the stars. I suggest that these phenomena are all examples of the transliminal at work. We sometimes need to use our propositionally tempered good sense to avoid being carried away by them.

CHAPTER 14

Mystery and Originality

Some questions.

I am going to start this chapter by posing a couple of questions. The first one is about the relationship between the transliminal and physical matter. It is my hope that the previous two chapters suggest that human beings are governed as much as or more by the transliminal way of knowing than by ordinary logic. On the other hand, because ordinary logic is taken to be the norm, this is not fully recognised. However, the subject matter of those chapters was ideas and power, emotions and art. When it comes to hard physical reality that is surely where the laws of physics, arrived at through application of ordinary logic, hold sway! But is it always? What about miracles? What about paranormal phenomena? These are controversial concepts. They are hotly disputed. However, there is enough evidence around to suggest that they cannot be dismissed out of hand. My question is: how precisely does the transliminal interface with physical matter?

Another question; a sense of numinosity, power and mission was identified in Chapter Eight as characteristic of transliminal experience. The last two chapters suggest that creativity and originality enter the human sphere via the transliminal. Where do the power, creativity, and originality come from? I have suggested that the power collected by the ruler or other exalted being is somehow handed over or extracted from individuals. A lot of creativity could be understood as a reorganisation of the contents of the individual unconscious – the sort of filing that mundane dreams carry out. However, I am not sure that this can explain all originality and newness. In fact, I suspect that all newness must come via the transliminal.

The more restricted mode introduced by the propositional and relational working together is probably confined to recycling what is already there but the human capacity for the truly original needs to connect beyond those confines. Thomas Khun, author of 'The Structure of Scientific Revolutions', recognized this distinction in his philosophy of science when he identified a difference between 'normal science' and 'paradigm shift'. The paradigm shift occurs when the whole perspective changes and a completely new vista opens out. But where does this new vista come from? What is its source?

Let me be honest. I do not intend to answer these questions in any straightforward manner. That is because I do not know the answers. I just think that they are interesting and important questions that point us to the limits of what we know and perhaps of what is knowable. These things are mysteries. They exist at the threshold, on the edge between the two ways of knowing. That edge has always held a powerful fascination.

Here is an example of that fascination. In the later 1960s, when the world was young and I was too, I spent a lot of time with mathematical physicists at Cambridge (despite the fact that I am borderline innumerate). This was because I was going out with and then married one. Were we a million miles apart, the student of the transliminal topic of medieval history and the soundly propositionally grounded mathematicians? Not so. Two dominant topics excited those young minds. One was how to quantize relativity - how to reconcile the incompatible information that physics was producing about the very small and the very large. The other was the search for the ultimate, smallest particle; the very basis of all matter. Forty years on neither of these goals has been reached. Quantum mechanics and relativity have both been significantly developed, but not reconciled, and however great the resources poured into the construction of ever larger particle accelerators, there is still no sighting of the ultimate fundamental particle. The Holy Grail or philosopher's stone remains just as far away.

Looking back on that time, and the excitement generated by the sense of being on the brink of uncovering the ultimate secrets of the universe, I now see the endeavour as thoroughly transliminally driven. It does not look so different from the project of the alchemists - except that there was a more sophisticated ambiguity about what the alchemists were up to. Were they trying to turn base metal into gold, or was this a metaphor for the transformation of the human being, as Jung and others powerfully suggest? The same sort of ambiguity between the physical and the spiritual hangs around the various magic practices, briefly introduced at the end of the previous chapter. Ambiguity is one hallmark of 'both-and' logic.

We are drawn to the place where known and unknown meet. We might know absolutely nothing about the unknown, but, my goodness, we are fascinated by that boundary between the known and the unknown; between matter and spirit. The boundary experiences of birth and death are obvious points of encounter with mystery. Here are horizons beyond which our logical minds cannot reach, and yet...

It is the same with visions of people who have recently died; ghosts; communication with the dead; past life and rebirth experiences - can all this data simply be binned because it rarely behaves properly when subjected to sustained experimental scrutiny? In fact there is some quite solid evidence for many of these phenomena. The problem as far as science is concerned is not so much lack of data as lack of an accepted and acceptable explanatory framework. There are other facets of life where matter and spirit appear to bump into each other, which never fail to fascinate. Paranormal phenomena such as telepathy come into this category. The shelf space in your local bookshop devoted to the esoteric and paranormal gives solid evidence of that fascination. It will be considerably more extensive than the psychology section!

In this chapter, I will illustrate these puzzles with a couple of examples of the encounter with mystery. The first tackles the puzzle of originality, and the second is for me about as close as you can get to the interface between matter and spirit. They come from opposite ends of the millennium that has just ended. The one at the beginning is a book, the Apocalypse of Beatus from the 9th Century, and the one at the end is a building, Gaudi's Sagrada Familia from the early 20th Century.

I introduced the idea just now that newness and coming into being is the province of the transliminal. As a student of cultural history, I was always fascinated by newness. We are all too familiar with cultural recycling; with 'retro'. However, since the boundaries of the aesthetically possible were blown wide open about one hundred and fifty years ago, we have also become jaded with experiment for the sake of experiment. True originality and newness has a transliminal edge to it. It connects at a visceral level. It produces a shiver down the spine. By taking an example from the early middle ages, I am well clear of the contemporary drive to produce the outrageous and unexpected. We are dealing here with a very different age; one whose artistic expression was normally bounded by tradition.

The Apocalypse of Beatus – the transliminal breaks through.

Let me take you down the centuries to a monastery in the Picos d'Europa Mountains in Northern Spain in the 9th Century, in pursuit of a manuscript that played a crucial part in the Renaissance of the 12th century. The Early Middle Ages were not a particularly good time for communications. After a few centuries of neglect, the Roman roads were no longer what they used to be and times were lawless, so that it was safer to stay put.

Most people did. Staying put has a restricting effect on the spread of learning and culture, and it was only when things got more settled and a critical mass of people started moving around again, that the Western European cultural flowering of the 12th Century Renaissance was possible. This comprised an explosion of creativity and learning in all departments. I am picking an example from architecture.

As historians trace the beginnings of the confident new vision found in architecture and architectural ornamentation in the early 12th Century, three sculptures are frequently cited. These tympana, or relief sculptures over the doors of churches, are found in three different places in France, at Autun, Vezelay and Moissac. They are similar to each other, but strikingly original in the context of everything that had gone before. They are recognized as the beginning of a whole new approach to church art and sculpture; a new confidence in monumental sculpture that had not been seen since Roman times, and which was soon to be taken much further. All three show a particularly powerful and energetic depiction of Christ in Majesty, surrounded by the strange beasts of the Apocalypse. (The Apocalypse is another name for the Revelation of St. John the Divine - the last book in the New Testament of the Bible.) The Apocalypse is a powerfully mystical and incomprehensible work that has inspired mad prophecies all down the centuries, as well as great art.

In tracing the origins of the new artistic phenomenon, represented by these tympana, the art historian Emile Male noted the influence of one 9th Century manuscript, the Apocalypse of Beatus. Before the days of printing, manuscripts were written and drawn on parchment, and laboriously copied by hand, usually by monks in monasteries. Where a work struck a chord, as Beatus's undoubtedly did, many copies would be made, and indeed, the surviving examples of this manuscript are all copies - the original eludes us. Because of the poor communications noted above, even the copies took about three centuries to filter through from the Picos Mountains of Spain to Southern and then central France, but filter through they did, and with notable impact. I first saw the copies of the manuscript as we chanced to holiday in the resort town of Potes just below Beatus's monastery, when there just happened to be a special exhibition of the manuscripts (coincidences are the speciality of the transliminal). This was thirty years after I had specialized in the 12th Century Renaissance, as part of my original, history, degree.

Once I saw them, I could appreciate how the images they contained had made such a momentous impression. The impact of Beatus's pictures was immediate, with their often menacing lines; their uncompromising broad areas of colour; black, red, gold-yellow. The angels are particularly striking with their spiky black, geometrical wings. With a gasp of recognition I saw those wings on the birds of prey that circled around Beatus's mountain home.

As you would expect of illustrations of the Apocalypse, the images are through and through archetypal. A word about archetypes, Carl Gustav Jung, one of the founders of psychoanalysis, and the one most interested in both spirituality and madness, used the term to describe powerful and universal images, or rather, more than images that are encountered in the unconscious mind; in my terms, the transliminal. According to Jung, the unconscious is collective - shared among the human race as well as accessible to individuals, chiefly in dreams and visions. These images have power - power to transform and to destroy. Normally they reside in the hidden world of our dreams, but they can break into the open, sometimes with explosive force. Beatus's pictures hit me with just such force.

I am recounting a powerful personal experience, but one that I know was shared, over the centuries, because of the way that that manuscript was copied and inspired the art of the 12th Century Renaissance throughout Europe. Little is known about Beatus. In contrast to my other example of Gaudi, to follow below, there is no suggestion that he flirted with madness, but he was undoubtedly a channel for powerful transliminal material which could have rocked a weaker individual. On the other hand, some of the lives of the saints, and of holy men in other parts of the world today, lead me to reflect, that, with the benevolent support of a good monastery or bunch of devoted followers, quite a lot of deficiencies or lapses in motivation over daily living skills can be covered up. Strange ideas, voices and visions in such a context are a bonus - they add to the credentials of sanctity.

Beatus himself has merged into the mists of history. His images live and have had a powerful and lasting effect on European culture. I would argue that that power is drawn via the transliminal.

The interface between the material and the spiritual: Sagrada Familia

My second example, Gaudi's Sagrada Familia, is also an example of originality. However, I am including it as it appears to me to illustrate about the closest encounter between the spiritual and the physical that I have come across. So, let us now travel in the imagination to Barcelona. The Sagrada Familia - the impossible cathedral - was the final work of the accomplished and highly original Catalan architect, Antonio Gaudi. Gaudi had proved his credentials in his craft by creating a number of striking, beautiful and perfectly practical buildings, such as apartment blocks, a church and a palace, in and around Barcelona. He understood the practicalities of realizing highly improbable buildings in bricks, mortar, stone or whatever, and provided he could persuade someone to believe in them and to pay for them, they got built. His faithful patrons, the wealthy arms dealers the Guells, were useful here.

During the last decades of his life, despite a huge reputation, his productivity gradually ground to a halt as he immersed himself in the task of designing and building his masterpiece, the Sagrada Familia. This was conceived not as a mere building project, but as a movement for spiritual revival. The conception laid out in his plans literally soared to unimagined heights. However, the situation on the construction site was rather different. The façade, with its strange towers, and some of the nave got partially built, and at a steadily decreasing pace. Gaudi left his comfortable home and came to live in a shed on the building site, totally absorbed in his dream. Progress with the construction was in inverse proportion to this absorption. Instead of concentrating on useful things like getting on with the nave, he was immersed in the symbolism of the numbers derived from the dimensions of the pillars. When an elderly and disheveled man was delivered to a Barcelona hospital in 1926, having been run over by a tram, and dying shortly afterwards of his injuries, his identity was discovered to be that of the great Gaudi.

In construction project terms, the Sagrada Familia in 1926 could be seen as one of the more spectacular failures of all times - worthy of an entire TV series in the great disasters genre, designed to make us feel smug about our own relative efficiency in getting things done. But: the incomplete Sagrada Familia is a defining monument for Barcelona and far beyond. Work is now gathering pace to realize the unrealizable; to turn dream and vision into stone and concrete. The necessary technology that was not there in Gaudi's day is now to hand. The absurdly extravagant cost of all this is met by money that the visitors to the unfinished monument pour into its coffers, in response to the majesty of that vision. Gaudi himself is on a fast track to sainthood through the arcane workings of the Roman Church.

Contemplating the façade that Gaudi never completed, you see the physicality of walls and towers dissolve into fantasy in the intricate coloured ceramic work over the lintel. He poured more and more of his effort into this essentially decorative feature, leaving the bulk of the structure as sketches, probably unrealizable within the limits of the technology of his day - and yet it is this ceramic work that seems to dissolve the solidity of the façade into transcendence; to make the bridge between earth and heaven. Sagrada Familia is a concrete monument to the intersection of physicality and fantasy; of solid ecclesiastical architecture and spiritual vision. Its impact on tourist and faithful alike redeems it from the status of mad folly. They might arrive as spectators at a curiosity; they become pilgrims and devotees. In common with many others, the experience moved me to tears.

I am very interested in this particular emotional response. I see it as the human response to mystery; to the meeting of matter and spirit; the reaching beyond the knowable into the unknown. I see it as the same response that Rudolf Otto grappled with as he sought to pin down the idea of The Holy, and came up with the concept of numinosity. Great art, music, architecture etc. operate at that intersection between matter and spirit. It is a response that can translate into impulsive generosity - into hard cash. The Gothic cathedrals that sprang up in competition with each other all over Europe in the high Middle Ages also represented a lot of hard cash poured into a spiritual enterprise. Gaudi was following the tradition of the builders of these cathedrals.

The medieval cathedral builders had less access to technical sophistication than did Gaudi in the early 20th Century - they managed to keep their improbable structures up by a system of balance and counter balance - constructing ribbed roofs with pointed arches to transfer the weight of their masonry to the outside walls, then adding more buttresses on the outside if this transferred force threatened to cave the walls outwards. Balance is crucial for the outcome of the encounter with mystery. Awe and imbalance are near neighbours; beyond the boundaries of logic there are dangers, precisely because there are no boundaries. Stray too far, and the route back will have dissolved. That way madness lies.

The example of Gaudi is interesting here too. In terms of getting on with the job and designing and finishing a church, complete with useful features like a roof, he totally failed to deliver. Lack of time was not the problem - he spent about thirty years with gradually increasing total absorption in the project. Admittedly, there were cash flow problems, but sponsors might have been a little put off by the rate of progress. Gaudi further slipped somewhat in terms of managing daily life. I suspect the Community Psychiatric Nurse might have labeled his saintly self denying regime as symptoms of self neglect. And yet... putting people, things, anything, into categories is such a basic human instinct. Gaudi will soon acquire one of the most exalted categories anyone can attract - that of a Catholic saint. However, in another context, could the same conduct attract early retirement from employment on health grounds, and/or a diagnosis of mental disorder? I do have a sneaking sympathy for his assistants and workers on the building project. It must have been a frustrating job.

Having explored the transliminal in both its dubious and its positive aspects in these three chapters, it is now time to return to God.

CHAPTER 15

About God

No one's slave

No-one's slave, I am no-one's master
No-one's slave, I am no-one's master,
On my grave they will write this after
I am gone
I will be gone.
And then my flesh will go to the earth it lived on
Breath will go to the air it lived from
I am through with the shame of my lying
Had my fill of the cruelty and crying
Earned my keep in the land where the dying
deserts grow.
And now I know
And I am looking out with a new perspective
Listening out for a new directive
Going back to the land of our mothers
I will walk with my sisters and brothers
We will share what is good with each other
In our love
It is a love
It is a love that brings you the invitation
Join me now in my invocation
Mother Earth I was nearly the end of you
Please accept my desire to be friends with you

Now I know just how much I depend on you
for life
You are my life
You are the life that grows in the flesh I'm weaving
Life that blows in the air I'm breathing
I am strong as a tree on a mountain
Full and fresh as a free flowing fountain
Bright and clear as the stars beyond counting
in the night
I am their light
I am the light that shines in a thousand people
In my sight every life is equal
No-one's slave, I am no-one's master
No-one's slave, I am no-one's master
On my grave they will write this after
I am gone
After I'm gone, After I'm gone,
I will be gone.

Theo Simon. 'Seize the Day'. From the CD 'Alive'.

Before tackling the mystery that is God, it is necessary to tackle that other mystery; death. Whereas there is a debate about the existence of God, death is an absolute certainty. Some would say that it is a depressing certainty. Undoubtedly, the loss of those close to us, those people who are part of the fabric of our being, is a painful facet of human existence.

On the other hand, death has an exhilarating aspect, well captured in Theo Simon's song, quoted at the beginning of this chapter. The triumphant phrase: 'I will be gone' is the signal to put the rest of life into a cosmic context; a context that brings moral obligations ('mother earth, I was almost the end of you, please accept my desire to be friends with you.'). At the same time, the song introduces that sense of the wider and wider web of connectedness, discussed in the chapter about relationship earlier. The sense of individual finiteness is juxtaposed with the infinitude of the whole of humanity, the whole of life, and of the stars in the heavens. Death makes sense of life. Death makes life glorious. 'No-one's Slave' succeeds in capturing this much in the space of one song, and makes Theo Simon my favourite theologian.

But hang on; didn't I claim to be a Christian? Is this song not a blatant smack in the face for the Christian idea of eternal life? I will here step into a minefield and declare that this is a matter of interpretation of words and concepts, and a good illustration of the way in which transliminal and everyday knowledge, the two incompatible ways of knowing, can trip each other up.

The crucial thing to hold onto (in the midst of the logical quick-sands) is the loss of categories and boundaries in the transliminal. Time and space are the basic categories that bound our everyday existence. Both dissolve in the transliminal. The idea of eternity being an *eternal now* is very old. The Greek philosopher, Plato, famously defined time as being 'A moving image of eternity' in his dialogue, 'The Timmaeus'. Boethius, a later classical philosopher, writing his 'Consolations of Philosophy' in the 5th Century CE, (while in prison, awaiting execution), picks up this definition and writes: 'Nunc stans facit aeternitatem' - something like 'The standing *now* makes eternity, whereas the moving *now* makes time.'(Italics added to try and make something rather subtle a bit clearer).

My view is as follows, and I stress that this is just my theory. The idea of eternal life for the individual after death is a fallacy based on misunderstanding the logic of the transliminal. Since transliminal, or symmetric, logic is based on 'both-and', by accessing the transliminal we can experience eternity, and indeed heaven, (or hell) within the confines of ordinary life. The accounts of our journeyers witness to that. It can happen in a short space of ordinary time too, as is well attested in the spiritual literature.

That is how I choose to interpret the sayings of Jesus in the Christian gospels concerning eternal life, while accepting that this could be a minority view. I also appreciate that Jesus was operating in a cultural context where there were ideas of supernatural places, like 'sheol' where people ended up after death, and the gospels relate controversy about the existence of resurrection (Mark12: 18 – 28, and Luke 20: 27 – 40) which Jesus deals with in his usual enigmatic fashion.

So much for survival of the individual; that unique history of propositional and relational working together during the span of a particular lifetime. However, as indicated earlier, I consider the individual to be only one part of a human being. I consider that the part that exists in connection, and is a part of and partaker of the web of other beings is eternal (but not individual!) The knowledge of the finiteness of the self and the life I am now living is tempered by my consciousness of being a part of that glorious whole – and my wish to be a worthy, albeit vanishingly tiny part.

Faith for me is believing that whole is good, and meaningful – taking the vision of Julian and so many others who have tapped deeply into the transliminal wisdom to heart. Love is the ultimate principle and 'All shall be well. All manner of things shall be well.' That this flies in the face of plenty of evidence to the contrary in the here and now is yet another 'both - and'.

I see this discussion as an essential precondition to getting to grips with God. There is a telling criticism of Christianity, and of the many other religions which prescribe an afterlife, by those who would see religion abolished. It claims that such faiths are simply a denial of death; a refusal to face that finality of death and a clinging on to our individual survival. I have a lot of sympathy with this criticism. However, I stressed earlier that the understanding I outlined above of eternal life, which I hold to be compatible with a gospel based Christianity, is just a theory. I make no claim to *know* what happens after death.

I am sure there are manifold theological objections to this

theory, but as I am not a theologian, and have no intention of becoming one, I will have to let that pass. I am aware of the literature on near death experiences, reincarnation and afterlife experiences, and the startling regularities and evidence that these claim. They certainly convince me that death does not lead to an immediate dissolution of the individual self; they reinforce my collection of evidence that psychic contents can transfer between minds – compatible with the idea that the billiard ball mind is a fallacy. However, such accounts do not convince me of the existence of the traditional Christian and Islamic type of idea of heaven (or hell). Rather, I respect the ultimate mystery of both life and death. I am simply not in a position to do more than speculate on such matters. Neither, in my opinion, is anyone else.

So, we do not need the idea of God as an opt out clause for death. Do we need God at all? I am here going to make a distinction between the concept of God and the experience of God. A concept is only possible when the propositional and relational work together to get a precise understanding of things. As God is, by any definition, simply off the radar of the propositional and relational working together, conceptualizing God is at least problematic, as discussed much earlier in this book. God is in the province of the transliminal, and the transliminal knows by experience, not by conceptualization. My suggestion is that we know about God through a particular quality of experience of relationship.

The Web of Relationship again.

Let us return to the theory that we human beings partly exist in concentric circles of relationship, and our being is mingled with important others. We have tracked those circles through important others, less important others, ancestors and descendants, our tribe and nation, the human race, the animal kingdom and the earth. Who is to say where that web ends or begins? To support this argument, I call on two sources of evidence. The first

is open to all of us, the second only to those travellers who have
ventured far into the transliminal and returned with their tales of
the journey.

To address the more generally available evidence; we all know
about relationship from the feeling and the information this
feeling gives us. The baby knows whether it is loved or
unacceptable from the reaction of those around it. Being loved
makes us feel alright. Feeling special is a universal longing if
nothing else. Where does that sense of specialness, or that sense
that we have a right to be special that all people seem to harbour
somewhere (usually well hidden from polite society) stem from?

I ponder this when, as a therapist, I work with people who
have been appallingly abused from an early age. They react with
anger. Even if their perceptions are so distorted that they blame
themselves for what happened, another part of them knows that
it was not right. They know that they are worth more than this.
They had a right to be treated with respect and not to be used.

All human beings have that right. I suggest that this sense
comes directly from that relationship which we can feel with that
which is deepest, widest, most all embracing. As this is far beyond
the range of our propositional minds, it is beyond words. The
propositional has all the words. So, one might as well call it God
as anything else. As I understand it, God survives because people
know him/her/it through relationship: this relationship is simultaneously situated at the widest and deepest point of the web of
relationship that is partly us. Logic is out of its depth here.

Then there are those who have ventured sufficiently far from
their individual selves to have felt in communion with the whole;
who have embraced that circle of the web; who have felt
themselves to be indivisible with the whole – the unitive
experience that was discussed in the chapter on the Christian
mystics. This is characteristically received as an experience of love
and awe, but also of terror. When the individual enters this state
with a disturbed mind, the initial experience can be negative. In

the case of someone with a weaker sense of self, failure to return to the normal state of internal equilibrium means prolonged exposure to that transliminal state. The experience then often becomes persecutory, because ordinary life cannot be navigated without access to concepts and boundaries. I do not see that this detracts from the validity of the vision of those, such as Julian of Norwich whom I at least would credit with having glimpsed more of that ultimate reality, which we cannot by our very constitution, ever know completely.

A little Stocktaking

It's time to face the critics of religion, time to track what follows from all this; but first of all, a little stocktaking. Where have we got to? The book started by challenging two common assumptions; the primacy of rationality (or propositionally based, either - or logic, as we can now identify it) and the billiard ball mind. It is my hope that, by introducing the two central meaning making systems of ICS, and their tendency to get decoupled at crucial moments, the shakiness of these assumptions will now be much clearer.

The tension between religious and spiritual experience, and institutional religion was traced. This led onto the idea of the threshold of experience, beyond which the rational part of the mind cannot operate, but which can be accessed through experience. Beyond the threshold, I called the transliminal, and illustrated the concept with examples from the Christian contemplative literature. Then the three travellers in this strange region reported their experiences.

These accounts provided a wealth of detail with which to illustrate the characteristics of the transliminal. The ideas of schizotypy, variations between different people in openness to this way of experiencing came in here, as did symmetric logic, the paradoxical, 'both-and' logic of the transliminal. I then introduced Interacting Cognitive Subsystems in order to ground the idea of the two ways of knowing in the way in which our thinking systems are organised in cognitive science.

According to this model, we have access to two ways of experiencing because we have two higher order meaning making systems. When these two are not working together, we are left with the default option: the relational. This means we lose our ability to think logically and really sort things out, but are left with the rest – the emotional, connecting part of our cognitive apparatus. We gain access to a way of perceiving that was closed to us by the filtering function of the propositional. Everything can take on a supernatural, awe inspiring and sacred feel, and the self recedes or expands. However, if we hang around here too long we might lose our way. That way madness lies.

I then illustrated the way in which being prepared to open ourselves to new experience of relationship in a more ordinary fashion is a natural part of our growth as human beings. This is because we are, in an important sense, our relationships. We are also individuals, with individual self consciousness. That is again because of the two equal meaning making systems that govern our thinking, and so our way of grasping the world. We are always in two places at once – unless we are thoroughly over the threshold in the transliminal – in which case, who knows where we are?

Critics of religion and fundamentalists.

Failure to appreciate this double edged nature of knowing leads to a number of fallacies and dangers. First, there is the assumption that the logical, propositional route to knowledge about the world is the only one – the first of our two assumptions. This is the trap that those who argue that religion is a dangerous anachronism fall into. We have already noted the way that Richard Dawkins, who is prominent among such commentators at present, recognises the power of symmetric logic, only to label it as a pernicious 'meme'. Symmetric logic, the logic of the relational mind, and so the transliminal, does indeed work by association – as do art and poetry. I would argue that what Dawkins identifies as an aberration is in fact integral to our humanness.

Then there are those who do defend religion, but do so in a way that excludes the sense of the transliminal. They seem to be blind to the sense of the sacred. To them it must be just a word, not an experience. I have heard sermons from clerics, who should have known better, that came over like that. Robert Winston, in his book, 'The Story of God', does acknowledge the otherness of God, so does not fall into that trap. However, his work is an example of explaining religion by reference to rationality; the need to cope with the dissonance of death; the evolutionary advantage conferred; the sense of community. I am sure all that is very fair, but for me it leaves out the central reason for the survival of God: the compelling power of the transliminal, and that sense of relationship with that which is beyond. That sense is always present in some form because it is built into our make up. It is not necessarily labelled as God – but labels are not relevant in relational space.

Of course, where you lie on the schizotypy spectrum will determine how open you are to this other way of being, and how compelling it is for you. Some people embrace spirituality and mystery uncritically. They are prepared to disregard the wisdom of the propositional entirely when faced with the fascination of the transliminal. I regard this as yet another fallacy. I have several times in this book used the term 'authentic spirituality.' This might or might not be based in a faith tradition – though a worshipping community provided it is not extreme and cultish, is a good pointer to finding a grounded religious context. The other sign of a healthy spirituality can be summed up by the biblical phrase "By their fruits you shall know them." Compassionate and justice-bearing action in the world is the best sign of that authentic spirituality. Real relationship brings with it a sense of responsibility. Open yourself to love, and you find yourself with commitments.

Fundamentalism – a failure to understand the transliminal.

Problems arise with the general fragmentation of faith communities. More and more people find themselves with no obvious spiritual home. This leaves people still with their spiritual longing; that yearning after the transliminal that is written into our being, but with no clear route for its expression. Sometimes it is satisfied by uncritical and self focused movements, which are trivial rather than sinister. This void can also leave people open to manipulation by more dangerous cults. These characteristically cut people off from their natural sources of support and extract lots of money from them. In extreme cases, such as Jonestown, it can even lead to pressure to commit suicide and mass murder.

These examples point to the vulnerability that is a part of opening to the transliminal. It means an opening to influence; to being taken over – hence the ease with which cult leaders can hold sway. Larger religious movements are not immune from this danger. The sort of fundamentalism that purports to provide absolute answers is another major aberration that comes from failure to understand the logic of the transliminal and to appreciate the subtle balancing act that is the human being. Fundamentalist faiths harness the compelling power of the transliminal, and so are enormously attractive to their adherents. Claiming certainty is very attractive in an uncertain world. However, by claiming that they have absolute truth, sometimes to the extent of overriding respect for life, for the rights of others etc. they are falling into the trap of confusing the two logics.

The logic of the transliminal is symmetric logic. Two incompatible things can be absolutely true at the same time. That is not a basis for slaughtering your opponents because they don't agree with you. Either - or logic belongs in the propositional. It is perfectly legitimate to reject an academic paper because its results are conclusively refuted elsewhere. Interpretation of scripture is just not like that. It is not a table of logarithms to be consulted.

Rather, the great sacred books, whether the Qur'an, the Bible or the Gita, help to lead us from the mundane world of hard and fast facts towards the shimmering logic of the transliminal. Niel Douglas Klotz's marvellously rich exposition of scriptures, 'Desert Wisdom', for example, brings out this aspect. More mature religious thinking can cope with the sort of radical ambiguity that it is necessary to tolerate when dealing with the transliminal. Critics of religion such as Dawkins rightly, in my view, criticize fundamentalism, but fail to distinguish between that and healthier versions of faith.

We have already seen that religious movements do not have a monopoly on harnessing the power of the transliminal for their own ends. Political movements, nationalism, advertising – all these have tapped into the potential for manipulating people afforded by mastery of the transliminal. The more alert we are to the way in which the relational mind operates, and how the attraction of the transliminal can seduce us, the less open to manipulation we will be, whether by commercial interests, or political or religious power mongers.

Advertisers and others are here tapping into the power of the relational mind to transform or transfigure the ordinary into something with a super-ordinary, numinous, glow. This can have a positive or a negative feeling tone to it. There are examples of this in the accounts of transliminal journeying in Chapter Seven: Mama becoming the owl, and the way the people that Matthew met with were experienced as either angels or demons. In a more ordinary way, stories work because of this faculty of the mind.

Fairy stories have this aura of myth and magic, yet the plot usually boils down to the disadvantaged youngster making his/her way in the world and finding a partner. The success of books and films such as Lord of the Rings derive their power from this archetypal source. The list is endless. Once you become alert to this dimension of experience it is everywhere. However, it is well to remember that tricksterish quality of the transliminal.

Its unreliability as a guide has already been noted, as well its ability to switch things from the sublime to the banal, without warning. It might feel cosmically beneficent or evil. Just like dreams, it can easily teeter towards the banal. Balance and discernment is everything.

The transliminal and escape from the real world.

The final danger is to do with the attraction of the transliminal, and its power to seduce us away from the real world. I have hinted a number of times that the attraction of street drugs is their ability to fast track people into this other dimension of experience. Alcohol is well known for its capacity to disable the more rational part of the mind, along with sensible inhibitions. I am not a puritan. I sometimes like to dim my propositional with a glass or two of wine with a good meal. However, the part that drugs and immoderate alcohol consumption play in our contemporary culture points to a sickness in society.

I would diagnose this as a sickness in our relationship to the transliminal. We have dismantled many of the traditional ways of accessing what is sacred and holy through our communities. We no longer worship together (much). We no longer sing and dance together (much). We tend to live privatised and fragmented lives; glued to screens like the one before me, rather than relating with people. We are fashioned with an inbuilt longing for connection and a yearning towards the transliminal. While well aware that drugs and drunkenness are not the preserve of our present age (Sherlock Holmes liked his cocaine, and the 18th Century painter of London life, Hogarth, graphically chronicled the effects of gin in his time), I do see here evidence of a poverty of spirit.

Another form of escape from the real world into the transliminal is, of course, madness. Often in the setting where I work I see this being triggered by drug use. For many people who experience the sort of brief psychotic episodes described by Annabel and Matthew, they are only too glad to get back to normality. However, Annabel charts graphically the hopelessness induced by stigmatizing diagnosis, and the insensitive hospitalization and psychiatric treatment that can follow such episodes. Little wonder when some people in this situation opt (probably not that consciously) for the exciting and super real transliminal/psychotic world – even with paranoia and critical voices – in preference to the place society offers them. Continuing to take cannabis or amphetamines, for those vulnerable to such breakdown, is an efficient way of achieving this result. Discontinuing the prescribed medication can be another.

From Karl Marx onwards ('religion is the opium of the people') critics of religion have criticized it for being a drug that diverts people from effective action in the real world. From my definition of true religion and authentic spirituality, it will be evident that I see it as more likely to lead to than inhibit social action (but not violence). However, the type of two dimensional religion that purports to have all the answers in simplistic form, and does not offer a justice dimension, could well fall into Marx's category.

In conclusion... long, long ago, when I was a history teacher (very briefly, I am glad to say), a little boy asked a question that has stuck with me. I had just given a detailed description of the complexities of the political situation of a particular medieval monarch, and how he dealt with them. My exposition was probably over complicated for the age group (I was a very inexperienced History teacher). This pupil asked: "But, was he a good king, Miss?" You might be forgiven for asking something similar at this point. Is the transliminal a good thing or a bad thing? One minute you are painting it one way, another the next. What about God – is he there or not? You are being rather vague about that. What about science? You say you are a scientist, but a lot of the time you don't sound very scientific. And madness – are you saying that it is the same thing as spirituality or aren't you?

I am recognizing that I might well have led my readers from

clarity to confusion; from certainty to ambiguity. That is because I believe uncertainty and ambiguity are at the heart of the human condition. The myths in the third chapter taught that there was no happy ending; no easy answers. Human beings have striven over the centuries to achieve utopias – where has it got them? So far, here!!

I do hope that I have managed to clarify a bit which are the areas where we might be able to establish definite answers. That has to be only those areas that are firmly in the sphere of the propositional mind (working in concert with the relational). Where I judge something to be beyond the scope of the propositional, I have identified it as mystery and refused to be drawn further. This means that I do believe that science is important, and that we need to keep our rational minds on tap, even when we venture beyond them. On the other hand, I have attempted to shed some sort of light on mystery and the transliminal; to track its characteristics and warn of its dangers.

Above all, I hope I have conveyed respect for relational knowing, for associative, both - and logic, and for the validity of that which we can experience but cannot precisely know. I have floated the hypothesis that we are only partly individual; through our relational minds we are part of the whole. This brings responsibility and pain. It also brings wonder and joy. Living is a rich adventure because of it. And the deepest and widest of those circles of relationship which we both are, and are beyond us, is God or whatever label you choose.

Books CDs and Websites

For the sources of much of the research and ideas behind this book, see my edited volume:

Isabel Clarke, (Ed.) 'Psychosis and Spirituality: exploring the new frontier'. London: Whurr Publishers Ltd. 2001

For more on the idea of two different ways of knowing that recurs throughout this book, see:

C. Clarke, (Ed). 'Ways of Knowing: science and mysticism today.' Exeter: Imprint Academic. 2005

For my other publications, and in order to access the (closed) yahoo discussion list about psychosis and spirituality, see my website:

www.scispirit.com/Psychosis_Spirituality/

For more information about the Spiritual Crisis Network (in the UK) see:

www.SpiritualCrisisNetwork.org.uk

Annabel Hollis's email (for talks): annabelhollis@hotmail.com

Books referred to

This is not a comprehensive reference list (for that, see my other publications), but I here list the more important sources referred to and relevant to this discussion.

For an accessible introduction to George Kelly and Construct theory:

Bannister, D. & Fransella, F. 'Inquiring Man.' Harmondsworth: Penguin. 1971

C.G. Jung. 'Modern Man in Search of a Soul'. London: Routledge. 2001

C.G. Jung. 'Memories, Dreams, Reflections'. London: Collins. 1962.

Matthew Fox. 'Original Blessing' Santa Fe, New Mexico: Bear & Co. 1983.

Naomi Klein. 'No Logo'. London: Flamingo(Harper Collins) 2001.

'The Cloud of Unknowing'. Anon. Edited by Evelyn Underhill. London:John M. Watkins. 1917.

Julian of Norwich. 'Revelations of Divine Love.' London: Hodder & Stoughton. 1987

St. John of the Cross. 'Selected Writings'. London: SPCK. 1987.

Peter Chadwick. 'Schizophrenia the Positive Perspective'. London: Routledge. 1997.

Stanislav and Christina Grof. 'The Stormy Search for the Self'. San Francisco: Harper Collins

Neil Douglas Klotz. 'Desert Wisdom' London: Thorsons (Harper Collins) 1995.

Andrew Jordan 'The Mute Bride'. Exeter: Stride. 1998.

Teasdale, J. & Barnard P. 'Affect, Cognition and Change.' Hove: LEA 1993.

The Opposition

Richard Dawkins 'The Selfish Gene'. Oxford. OUP. 1976.

Richard Dawkins 'The God Delusion' London: Bantam Books. 2006.

Christopher Hitchens 'God is not great'. London: Atlantic Books. 2007.

Stephen Jay Gould. 'Rock of Ages'. New York: Ballantine Books. 1999.

Robert Winston. 'The Story of God'. UK: Transworld Publishers Ltd. 2006

CDs

Robb Johnson. '21st Century Blues'. Irregular Records. IRR043
Robb Johnson. 'Overnight'. Irregular Records. IRR027
Robb Johnson. 'The Night Café'. Irregular Records. IRR025
Seize the Day. From the CD 'Alive', www.seizetheday.org

BOOKS

O books
O is a symbol of the world, of oneness and unity. In different cultures it also means the "eye", symbolizing knowledge and insight, and in Old English it means "place of love or home". O books explores the many paths of understanding which different traditions have developed down the ages, particularly those today that express respect for the planet and all of life.

For more information on the full list of over 300 titles please visit our website
www.O-books.net

SOME RECENT O BOOKS

The Celtic Wheel of the Year
Celtic and Christian Seasonal Prayers
Tess Ward

This book is highly recommended. It will make a perfect gift at any time of the year. There is no better way to conclude than by quoting the cover endorsement by Diarmuid O'Murchu MSC, "Tess Ward writes like a mystic. A gem for all seasons!" It is a gem indeed.
Revd. John Churcher, Progressive Christian Network

1905047959 304pp £11.99 $21.95

Gays and the Future of Anglicanism
Andrew Linzey and Richard Kirker

This book breathes toleration. It invites thought. It abhors the polemical. It is very Anglican - in the best sense - in that it tries to bring under-standing, be inclusive and avoid expulsion. Yet it has authority, without being bossy and authoritarian. Readers will find much to chew on to help them think about what is the nature of church for which they strive. "Gays and the Future of Anglicanism" is about much more than homosexuality and is highly recommended.
RENEW

190504738X 384pp £17.99 $29.95

A Global Guide to Interfaith
Reflections From Around the World
Sandy Bharat

This amazing book gives a wonderful picture of the variety and excitement of this journey of discovery.
Rev Dr. Marcus Braybrooke, President of the World Congress of Faiths

1905047975 336pp £19.99 $34.95

God in the Bath
Relaxing in the Everywhere Presence of God
Stephen Mitchell

This little book is destined to become a spiritual classic...A wonderfully refreshing and invigorating reading of Christianity.
Nigel Leaves, author of *Odyssey*

1905047657 112pp £9.99 $19.95

God Without God
Western Spirituality Without the Wrathful King
Michael Hampson

Writing with an admirable lucidity and following a tight line of argument, Michael Hampson outlines a credible Christian theology for the twenty-first century. Critical at times of both evangelical and catholic traditions, of both liberal and conservative thinking, he seeks to make faith accessible to those for whom established forms of belief have

become inappropriate in the present-day context.
Canon David Peacock, former Pro-Rector, University of Surrey

9781846941023 256pp £9.99 $19.95

Gospel of Falling Down
The beauty of failure, in an age of success
Mark Townsend

It's amazing just how far I was drawn into Mark's words. This wasn't just a book but an experience. I never realized that failure could be a creative process.
Editor, '*Voila*' Magazine

1846940095 144pp £9.99 $16.95

Liberal Faith in a Divided Church
Jonathan Clatworthy

This is a truly radical book, in that it looks for the roots of a liberal approach to Christianity that is principled, inclusive and undogmatic. Jonathan Clatworthy shows how liberal faith has always striven to temper the wisdom of the past with the promptings of the Spirit in the present. Rather than seeing such an approach as a departure from true orthodoxy, he demonstrates that they lie at the heart of a consistent vision of God's relationship with the world. This book will provide encouragement and sustenance for those who wish for an alternative to absolute certainty, in its secular and religious forms.
Elaine Graham, Professor of Social and Pastoral Theology, University of Manchester

9781846941160 272pp £14.99 $29.95

Life in Paradox
The Story of a Gay Catholic Priest
Paul Edward Murray

This memoir is the compelling story of an honest, sensitive priest, and the tragic tale of a hierarchy that has lost its way in its desire to control the Church rather than nurture it. No book sets out more clearly and urgently the tragedy and the prospects of the current crisis of Catholicism.
Bruce Chilton, Bernard Iddings Bell Professor of Religion, Bard College

9781846941122 240pp **£11.99 $24.95**

Peace Prayers
From the World's Faiths
Roger Grainger

Deeply humbling. This is a precious little book for those interested in building bridges and doing something practical about peace.
Odyssey

1905047665 144pp **£11.99 $19.95**

Thinker's Guide to Evil
Peter Vardy

As a philosopher of religion Peter Vardy is unsurpassed.
John Walter, Dialogue Magazine

1903816335 192pp **£9.99 $15.95**

The Way of Thomas
John Mabry

Compelling and well-written, this book will broaden the Jesus debate of our century.
John Shelby Spong, author of *The Sins of Scripture*

1846940303 196pp £10.99 $19.95

Other Prayers of Jesus
John Henson

To read John Henson is always to look at things from a fresh angle. Sometimes with a jolt, he opens up new and earthy glimpses of God's grace.
Peter West, Christian Aid area co-ordinator

9781846940798 176pp £11.99 $24.95

Adjust Your Brain
A Practical Theory for Maximising Mental Health
Paul Fitzgerald

Fascinating, enthralling, and controversial. Paul Fitzgerald's theories of brain functioning and mental illness are certain to capture the attention of the lay person and the esteemed scientist alike. Regardless of your opinion of his ideas, this book is certain to do one thing: make you think very deeply about your perceptions, your emotions, your moods, and the very nature of what it is to be human... and about our abilities to alter these through the use of psychopharmacology.
Dr. Ryan K. Lanier, PhD, Behavioral Pharmacologist, Johns Hopkins University School of Medicine

978-1-84694-0 224pp £11.99 $24.95

Back to the Truth
5000 years of Advaita
Dennis Waite

This is an extraordinary book. The scope represents a real tour de force in marshalling and laying out an encyclopaedic amount of material in way that will appeal both to the seasoned and to the introductory reader. This book will surely be the definitive work of reference for many years to come.
Network Review

1905047614 600pp £24.95 $49.95

Is There an Afterlife?
David Fontana

It will surely become a classic not only of parapsychology literature in general but also of survival literature in particular.
Radionics
Winner of the Scientific and Medical Network prize

1903816904 496pp £14.99 $19.95

Science of Oneness
Malcolm Hollick

A comprehensive and multi-faceted guide to the emerging world view. Malcolm Hollick brilliantly guides the reader intellectually and intuitively through the varied terrains of the sciences, psychology, philosophy and religion and builds up a vibrant picture that amounts to a new vision of reality for the 21st century. A veritable tour de force.

David Lorimer, Programme Director, Scientific and Medical Network

1905047711 464pp £14.99 $29.95

The Fall
Steve Taylor

"The Fall" is one of the most notable works of the first years of our century, and I am convinced it will be one of the most important books of the whole century.
International Journal of Transpersonal Studies

1905047207 352pp £12.99 $24.95

The Last of the Shor Shamans
Alexander and Luba Arbachakov

The publication of Alexander and Luba Arbachakov's 2004 study of Shamanism in their own community in Siberia is an important addition to the study of the anthropology and sociology of the peoples of Russia. Joanna Dobson's excellent English translation of the Arbachakov's work brings to a wider international audience a fascinating glimpse into the rapidly disappearing traditional world of the Shor Mountain people. That the few and very elderly Shortsi Shamans were willing to share their beliefs and experiences with the Arbachakov's has enabled us all to peer into this mysterious and mystic world.

Frederick Lundahl, retired American Diplomat and specialist on Central Asia

9781846941276 96pp **£9.99 $19.95**

Who on EARTH was JESUS?
the modern quest for the Jesus of history
David Boulton

What happens when the Christ of faith meets the Jesus of history? This is the question that preoccupies Boulton in an amazingly good synthesis of historical Jesus scholarship. His scope is as wide-ranging as it is even-handed; from theologians to scholars to popes, he distills their thoughts into a comprehensible and comprehensive survey of the best of the contemporary thinkers. Readers will find no overt proselytizing in this book. Instead, the author treats them to an unbiased look at the ever-changing discipline of Jesus studies. In the end, Boulton understands that it is not the scholar, nor the theologian, who will define the kingdom on Earth. Rather, it will be the job of all of us to discern the Jesus of today from words written long ago. This book is not to be missed.
Publisher's Weekly

9781846940187 448pp **£14.99 $29.95**

Bringing God Back to Earth
John Hunt

Knowledgeable in theology, philosophy, science and history. Time and again it is remarkable how he brings the important issues into relation with one another... thought provoking in almost every sentence, difficult

to put down.
Faith and Freedom

1903816815 320pp **£9.99 $14.95**

Deep Equality
Living in the Flow of Natural Rhythms
Jocelyn Chaplin

For many years, Jocelyn Chaplin has worked at the cutting edge of therapy, politics and conscious living. In this book she pulls together all the marvelous ideas and intuitions we have been hearing and experiencing at conferences and workshops. This is a text that academics, activists and anyone involved with the future of humanity should read, allowing themselves to become inspired by what Chaplin means when she writes of Deep Equality.
Andrew Samuels, Professor of Analytical Psychology, University of Essex

9781846940965 160pp **£9.99 $22.95**

God Without God
Western Spirituality Without the Wrathful King
Michael Hampson

Writing with an admirable lucidity and following a tight line of argument, Michael Hampson outlines a credible Christian theology for the twenty-first century. Critical at times of both evangelical and catholic traditions, of both liberal and conservative thinking, he seeks to make faith accessible to those for

whom established forms of belief have become inappropriate in the present-day context.
Canon David Peacock, former Pro-Rector, University of Surrey

9781846941023 256pp **£9.99 $19.95**

How to Meet Yourself
...and find true happiness
Dennis Waite

An insightful overview of the great questions of life itself: a compelling inner tapestry that encourages the reader to willingly embrace life being exactly as it is. Readable, relevant and recommended.
Chuck Hillig, author of *Enlightenment for Beginners*

1846940419 360pp **£11.99 $24.95**

Love, Healing and Happiness
Spiritual wisdom for secular times
Larry Culliford

This will become a classic book on spirituality...immensely practical and grounded. A nourishing book that lays the foundation for a higher understanding of human suffering and hope.
Reinhard Kowalski, Consultant Clinical Psychologist and author of *The Only Way Out Is In*

1905047916 224pp **£10.99 $19.95**